THE
Fresh & Healthy
INSTANT POT®
COOKBOOK

THE
Fresh & Healthy
INSTANT POT®
COOKBOOK

75 Easy Recipes for Light Meals to
Make in Your Electric Pressure Cooker

MEGAN GILMORE

TEN SPEED PRESS
California | New York

To my family—you inspire me to cook quick and healthy meals so I can spend more of my time with you!

Contents

Introduction

Let's face it, we all struggle to eat healthy, nutritious meals on busy weeknights. When you just have to get food on the table, it's easy to fall back on takeout, frozen meals, and other packaged convenience foods. That can add up quickly when you're on a budget, and this way of eating typically leaves me and my family feeling not so great. That's why I love the Instant Pot. It makes healthy cooking easier, so I can enjoy nutritious, homemade meals on a regular basis.

When I first got my Instant Pot, I found it slightly intimidating and used it mostly for cooking basic food staples, like batches of quinoa, rice, and dry beans. That alone saved me time and effort, but it wasn't until I discovered that I could cook two dishes at once, using the pot-in-pot method (see page 16), that I truly fell in love. Now, I can easily make a complete meal in less than an hour—with most of that time being totally hands-off. I love being able to accomplish other tasks around my house while a healthy meal cooks to perfection.

With an Instant Pot, fast and flavorful dishes are within reach no matter how hectic life gets. The quick-cooking power of the Instant Pot means there's no need to spend hours in your kitchen hovering over the stove. And because pressure cooking has proven to be one of the best options available for protecting the nutrients in your food, the Instant Pot is an ideal way to make healthy eating achievable.

Healthy Cooking with the Instant Pot

What is it about the Instant Pot that makes it so well suited for healthy cooking? Well, first of all, the pressurized pot lowers the boiling point of water, so your food is rarely cooked at a temperature above 250°F. Since cooking at high temperatures can reduce the nutrients present in food after cooking, it is thought that food cooked at lower temperatures may be more nutrient dense. Along the same lines, because the Instant Pot reduces your overall cooking time, food has less of a chance to lose its nutrients.

Another benefit of cooking with steam pressure is that it can intensify the flavors of your ingredients, and in some cases makes it unnecessary to sauté aromatic ingredients before you get started. That means you can use less oil, or even avoid it entirely, while cooking in the Instant Pot. As a result, this may reduce the total number of calories in your meals and aid in weight loss.

Since the Instant Pot cooks food 50 to 70 percent faster than traditional cooking methods, it may also save you energy in the kitchen—with regard to both your own physical efforts and your home's electrical usage. It's considered a green energy choice, requiring less energy than your stove, oven, or even a slow cooker. You could save on your home's cooling bills, too, because the Instant Pot won't overheat your house. How cool is that?

Pressure cooking also makes healthy eating more affordable and accessible because you can easily cook dry beans, legumes, and grains from scratch in a fraction of the time they would take on the stove. Buying these items in bulk tends to be less expensive, and making them at home allows you to avoid the preservatives and additives found in canned and packaged convenience foods.

Unlike traditional cooking, you can't open the Instant Pot during the cooking process to check on your ingredients, so it is even more important than usual to have a trusted and foolproof collection of recipes at your disposal. I have you covered there. All of these recipes have been carefully tested and retested to ensure your meals will turn out perfectly when you finally open the lid.

Keep in mind that using an electric pressure cooker doesn't always shorten the total cooking time, but it will certainly reduce the amount of time you spend in the kitchen actively cooking. You don't need to wait by the stove for water to boil, and you don't run the risk of burning the bottom of the pan when you get distracted for just a second, because the Instant Pot times everything for you.

When using an Instant Pot, you have to keep in mind the amount of time it takes for the pot to come to pressure before the pressure cooking cycle begins, and the amount of time it takes the pot to release that pressure after the pressure cooking cycle ends. Depending on the ingredients in your pot, the time to come to pressure is similar to waiting for water to boil. The time it takes to release pressure differs depending on whether a recipe calls for a quick release or a natural release (see page 16). All of these recipes list the total time it takes to make the dish, so you'll have a good idea of how many minutes it takes to prep the ingredients, bring the pot to pressure, cook the meal, and release the pressure. All of the times noted in this book are for a 6-quart Instant Pot, so if you're using an 8-quart pot, it may take several more minutes to pressurize, since that pot is larger. (As a result, vegetables tend to turn out softer when using this size pot, too.)

Having a realistic understanding of the time required to make each dish gives you the freedom to do something else—whether that's prepare the rest of your dinner, spend time with your family, or catch up on some laundry. While the food may not always be ready in an "instant," you'll definitely feel like the ultimate multitasker!

About the Recipes

I've developed all of the recipes in this book with optimum nutrition, flavor, and speed in mind. They call for easy-to-find, real-food ingredients that maximize your vitamin and mineral intake, while also taking calories into account, in case weight loss is one of your goals, too.

To make each meal as healthy as possible, I've included a generous serving of vegetables in every recipe. If you or someone you're cooking for isn't a vegetable lover (yet), the Instant Pot actually offers an advantage. Because pressure cooking tends to turn vegetables to mush if you cook them for too long, it's easy to sneak vegetables into your meals in unexpected ways. For example, rather than using a lot of heavy cream and an expensive blender to make a cream sauce, you can totally dissolve a head of cauliflower to create the creamy mac 'n' cheese sauce on page 118. And when you cook sweet potatoes in the same pot as the chocolate cake on page 184, the potatoes become a soft and creamy base for a rich, chocolate frosting to top the cake. Vegetables have never tasted so good!

If you have special dietary needs beyond just wanting to eat healthier, this book arms you with plenty of options. I've included gluten-free options for every single recipe that contains gluten, without the need for special gluten-free flour mixes, and all recipes are naturally sweetened (meaning there's no refined sugar) to help keep your blood sugar levels balanced, too.

If you follow a vegan or vegetarian diet, almost every recipe that calls for meat or fish also has a tested vegan substitute so you won't miss out on any delicious flavors. Nearly every sauce in the book is already vegan, so you can easily swap the protein to suit your needs, or use up any ingredients that you have on hand. If you *do* eat meat, try one of the meatless variations every now and then. It adds variety to your diet and helps you cut back on your weekly grocery bills.

Since dairy products can cause digestive issues for many people, I've also limited the use of dairy in these recipes. If you're in this camp, feel free to omit cheese when it is called for in a recipe, or use the vegan variations for a totally dairy-free dish.

No matter what your dietary needs are, you'll find plenty of healthy recipes to enjoy in this collection. To help you get started, I've included a list of my favorite pantry staples (page 7) and kitchen tools (page 11) to make shopping and cooking easier. If some of the ingredients in these recipes are unfamiliar, take a look at the ingredients and substitutions section on page 8 for some simple swaps. And if you've never used an Instant Pot before, check out my easy reference guide on page 15. It walks you through the operation of your pressure cooker and helps you troubleshoot the most common problems.

Let's get started!

My Go-To Pantry Staples

Because one of the goals of this book is to help you eat healthily as often as possible, I have purposefully developed these recipes using many of the same pantry staples over and over again. This helps me simplify my pantry storage and my shopping list at the same time.

By minimizing the number of ingredients you must keep on hand, you'll be able to locate key staples in your pantry faster and may be more likely to have what you need when you're ready to make dinner. Prepare to be amazed by the variety of flavors you can create with these go-to ingredients!

A list of my favorite—and often-used—pantry staples is below. Take this to your local grocery store and stock up. Once your pantry is filled, you will have everything you need to make the recipes in this book, and you shouldn't need to restock for several months.

VINEGARS, OILS, AND OTHER LIQUIDS

Apple cider vinegar (raw; see page 8)

Balsamic vinegar (aged, 4 percent acidity; see page 8)

Blackstrap molasses

Coconut oil (see page 10)

Maple syrup (see page 10)

Mustard: spicy brown and yellow

Olive oil (extra-virgin)

Sesame oil (toasted)

Soy sauce (or tamari; see page 10)

Sriracha (see page 10)

Vanilla extract

DRY GOODS: GRAINS, BEANS, AND FLOURS

Arrowroot starch (see page 8)

Barley (pearled)

Beans: black, garbanzo (chickpeas), kidney, and navy

Black-eyed peas

Buckwheat groats

Bulgur

Cacao powder (or cocoa powder)

Coconut sugar (see page 10)

Farro

Lentils: red and green

Millet flour (or whole grains for grinding)

Oat flour (see page 10)

Oats (quick-cooking)

Quinoa

Rice: long-grain brown, wild, wild and brown blend, and white jasmine

White whole-wheat flour (100 percent; see page 11)

DRIED FRUIT, NUTS, SEEDS, AND SPICES

Almonds (sliced)

Basil (dried)

Cayenne pepper

Chili powder

Cinnamon (ground)

Coriander (ground)

Cranberries (dried)

Cumin (ground)

Curry powder

Garam Masala

Garlic powder

Ginger (ground)

Oregano

Paprika

Pumpkin seeds (raw)

Raisins

Red pepper flakes

Sage (ground)

Salt (fine pink Himalayan)

Sesame seeds

Thyme (dried)

Turmeric

Walnuts

CANNED OR JARRED ITEMS*

Almond butter (see page 8)

Artichoke hearts

Beans: black, garbanzo (chickpeas), great Northern, and pinto

Chipotle peppers in adobo sauce

Peanut butter (all-natural)

Tomatoes, diced, with no added salt or sugar (see page 10)

Tomatoes, fire-roasted with green chiles (see page 10)

Tomato paste

Look for boxes or glass jars whenever possible to avoid the chemical BPA, which can be found in can linings.

Common Ingredients & Substitutions

I recommend that you first try the recipes as written to taste the intended result. But after that, please feel free to experiment with alternative ingredients and flavors. Here are some common items I use in my recipes with a few appropriate substitutes to help you achieve the best results possible.

Almond Butter: When almond butter is called for in a recipe, the only ingredient on the package label should be *almonds*. Avoid brands that contain additives like sugar or oil because those extras may interfere with your recipe results. You can also make your own almond butter by grinding almonds in a food processor for 15 to 20 minutes until creamy, or you can swap in all-natural peanut butter for slightly different results. (Peanut butter tends to make baked goods drier and less sweet.) To make a nut-free recipe, use sunflower seed butter instead of almond butter, but keep in mind that the sunflower seed butter will change the flavor somewhat and that baked goods that also call for baking soda will turn green, due to a safe chemical reaction. It's something to keep in mind for St. Patrick's Day!

Apple Cider Vinegar: I use vinegar to provide an acid flavor in recipes, and this is my favorite type of vinegar to use because it is thought to also help regulate blood sugar levels, lower cholesterol, and boost digestion. Look for raw apple cider vinegar "with the Mother" for the most health benefits, particularly in salad dressing recipes. If you can't locate this vinegar, freshly squeezed lemon juice is the best alternative.

Arrowroot Starch: This easily digested starch is used to thicken sauces, like in the Korean Chicken Bowls on page 106 and the Orange Chicken & Vegetables on page 156. Because it's a thickener, it is only added at the end of recipes and needs to be mixed with water to create a "slurry" that is more easily incorporated. Tapioca starch can be used as a substitute with similar results, or you can omit the starch entirely. When omitting the starch, I recommend turning on the Sauté function at the end of the recipe to simmer away any extra liquid and thicken the sauce slightly.

Balsamic Vinegar: Aged balsamic vinegar complements recipes with tomatoes perfectly and has a lower acidity level, making for a more mellow and balanced flavor. Look for balsamic vinegar with 4 percent acidity for the best results. Even though this type of balsamic is more expensive than others, a single bottle could last a year or more. If you can find only the less expensive varieties with 6 percent acidity, add a splash of maple syrup to the recipe to help balance out the extra acidity.

Coconut Milk: I use full-fat canned coconut milk, found in the Asian foods aisle of your grocery store, to replicate the texture of heavy cream. Canned coconut milk tends to separate when stored at a temperature of 76°F or below, but you can easily fix that by placing the unopened can in a bowl of very hot tap water for 10 minutes. Once warm, shake the can to mix the milk, then open it and measure out the amount needed for your recipe. Though it's less creamy, you can also use light canned coconut milk,

or the coconut milks sold in the refrigerated section, to lower the fat and calorie content in recipes.

Coconut Oil: Coconut oil has antibacterial properties and contains lauric acid, which is thought to help prevent high blood pressure and high cholesterol. Though I tend to use it sparingly, this oil is perfect for dessert recipes like puddings and frostings, which need to thicken when chilled. Choose extra-virgin coconut oil for the most nutrition, but refined coconut oil can be used when you don't want a hint of coconut flavor. If you don't care for coconut oil and can tolerate dairy, grass-fed butter or ghee make the best substitutes.

Coconut Sugar: Coconut sugar is a low-glycemic natural sweetener that can be used in place of granulated sugar for a slightly less-sweet result. I use coconut sugar when a dry sweetener is required for texture, like in the case of brownies or cakes. If you can't find coconut sugar, sucanat or brown sugar are the most similar substitutes.

Maple Syrup: Not to be confused with pancake syrup, which may have several additional ingredients on the label, 100 percent pure maple syrup is a natural sweetener produced from the sap of maple trees. It has a rich maple flavor and is perfect for sweetening vegan recipes. If you're not vegan, you may also use honey as a substitute for maple syrup. Keep in mind that honey is slightly sweeter than maple syrup so you may want to use slightly less than what is called for in a recipe.

Oat Flour (Gluten-Free): I love using oat flour for my gluten-free baking needs as it is affordable and readily available. If you have rolled oats in your pantry, you can make oat flour at home by simply grinding the oats in a blender, food processor, or coffee grinder. If you need to be gluten-free, be sure that your oats or store-bought oat flour are labeled "certified gluten-free" so you know there hasn't been any cross-contamination with gluten during processing.

Sea Salt: I use fine Himalayan pink salt in my recipes, as it contains essential minerals like calcium, magnesium, and iron. I like the Real Salt brand, but any fine sea salt would work well.

Sriracha: This is a spicy sauce made from red chile peppers and garlic. You can usually find it in the Asian foods aisle of your grocery store, where coconut milk and soy sauce are sold. If you can't locate it, use a dash of cayenne pepper in its place.

Tamari: A gluten-free soy sauce, tamari is great for boosting the flavor in a variety of recipes. If you don't need your food to be gluten-free, regular soy sauce can be used in its place. If you can't tolerate soy, you may also use coconut aminos as a soy-free substitute, but you'll have to add extra salt to the recipe to compensate for the difference in flavor. I use full-sodium tamari in my recipes for maximum flavor.

Tomatoes (Diced): When shopping for canned tomatoes, look for brands that have only one ingredient on the label: tomatoes. (Pomi and DeLallo brands are two good options.) If you can only find tomatoes with added salt or sugar, use less of those ingredients than the recipe calls for to ensure you wind up with the intended flavor.

Tomatoes (Fire-Roasted with Green Chiles): This canned mix of tomatoes and green chiles is used for making dishes with a Mexican-style flare, like tacos and queso dip. It can be found in the canned tomato section of your grocery store. The best substitute is a prepared medium-spicy salsa.

White Whole-Wheat Flour: This flour is made from 100 percent whole wheat, so it has the same nutritional value as traditional whole-wheat flour with a milder flavor and paler color. I prefer to use this type of flour when making healthier cakes and cookies, but you can also use certified gluten-free oat flour for a gluten-free alternative. I've included tested gluten-free variations for all of the recipes in this book for easy substitutions.

Best Kitchen Tools

As with my recipes, I like to keep my kitchen equipment as simple as possible. The following tools and cooking accessories are all you need to make every recipe in the book. Although some are specific to the Instant Pot, most of them are not and you may already have them in your kitchen. For easy shopping, I put links to everything here on my website. Check it out at https://detoxinista.com/instant-pot-accessories.

Bowl (7-inch): If you'd like to try pot-in-pot cooking, which means you cook one thing in the main pot and cook something else in a separate bowl set atop a trivet (see page 16), you need a 7-inch oven-safe bowl to fit easily into the Instant Pot. An oven-safe 4-cup bowl works well, or you can use a 7-inch round pan (see page 12) instead.

Handled Trivet: This is the trivet that comes with your Instant Pot, so you should already have it

stocked in your kitchen. I use this trivet often, and refer to it simply as the "handled trivet" in recipes.

Heat-Resistant Oven Mitts: The main pot and any additional cooking accessories (trivets, pans) get hot under pressure cooking, so you'll need some heat-resistant mitts to remove hot pans from the device. I recommend choosing a pair made of silicone for extra gripping power and heat protection.

Immersion Blender: To streamline my cooking and reduce the number of dirty dishes in the sink, I use an immersion blender to blend soups, gravies, and even puddings directly in the Instant Pot. If you don't have an immersion blender, you can use a standard blender for these recipes, but you may have to blend in batches. Always use caution, as the steam pressure from blending hot liquids can blow the lid off your blender.

Microplane Grater/Zester: I use this fine grater to quickly mince fresh garlic and ginger directly into the main pot, and also as a citrus zester.

Parchment Paper: I line my 7-inch round pan (see page 12) with parchment paper to guarantee easy removal of my finished baked goods. Don't bother trying to cut a perfect circle when lining your pans; if you press a square-shaped piece of paper into a round pan, the corners that go up the sides of the pan make easy handles for removing the final product. Lightly grease your pan before lining with parchment paper to help keep the parchment in place.

Plate (7-inch): You most likely already have a 7-inch oven-safe salad or side plate in your home, so there's no need to buy something special here. This is perfect for covering a 7-inch round pan (see below) during the cooking process to protect your baked goods from unwanted moisture. I prefer covering my food with this nontoxic and reusable option, rather than relying on aluminum foil.

Potato Masher: A potato masher is not only handy for mashing potatoes, but it can also help make cauliflower "rice" and "fried rice" (see pages 56 and 121) in a matter of minutes without using your food processor.

Round Pan (7-inch): To make cakes, brownies, and granola bars, you'll need a 7-inch pan that fits inside your Instant Pot. I like this size because it fits directly on the Instant Pot's handled trivet (see page 11), so it's easy to remove from the pot after cooking. An 8-inch pan will fit in the 8-quart Instant Pot, but the recipes in this book were designed for a 7-inch pan. Using a larger pan will give you more shallow results, and using a smaller (6-inch) pan will require a longer cooking time.

Steamer Basket: When you want to prepare steamed vegetables that don't touch the cooking water and can be easily removed from the pressure cooker, a steamer basket comes in handy. There are several brands specially designed to fit in the Instant Pot, or choose a classic steamer basket with an extendable handle so you can use it on the stove top, too.

Trivet (2.5-inch and 4-inch): If you'd like to try pot-in-pot cooking (see page 16), you'll need a trivet to keep the two dishes separate. I use a 2.5-inch trivet in most cases, but if you're making a large recipe, like Sneaky Sloppy Joes (page 168), or a double batch of any recipe, a 4-inch trivet gives you extra height. (The two are often sold as a two-piece set online.)

Widemouthed Mason Jars (8-ounce): Glass jars are great for recipes that are designed to be portable, like my Take-Along Veggie Frittatas (page 35), or for packing a lunch on the go. Four of these jars fit perfectly on the Instant Pot's handled trivet (see page 11) and can be stacked on top of each other to easily double a recipe.

HANDLED TRIVET

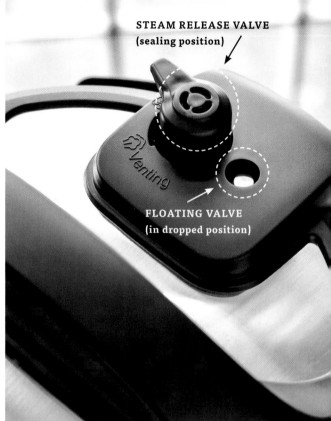

STEAM RELEASE VALVE
(sealing position)

FLOATING VALVE
(in dropped position)

STEAM RELEASE VALVE
(venting)

CHECKING THE SILICONE
SEALING RING

Your Instant Pot Resource Guide

If you've never used a pressure cooker before, here's what you need to know to get started right away. I've included photos for reference on the opposite page, but you can also refer to your machine's user manual for more details.

Before you start cooking:

Make sure the stainless-steel insert is clean and properly placed.

Every time I use my Instant Pot, I wipe the outside of the stainless-steel pot with a dry towel to make sure nothing has stuck to the bottom or sides after I've placed it on the counter or in my sink. Stuck-on food or debris can interfere with the functioning of your pot, so make sure it's clean each time you use it.

Check that the silicone sealing ring is properly seated in the lid.

When you use your Instant Pot, the silicone sealing ring expands from the heat and may move around when you take off the lid. Before securing the lid, use your fingers to gently wiggle the sealing ring all around the metal lid to ensure it is properly placed.

Make sure nothing is clogging the vent in your lid.

The stainless-steel cover over the vent is removable, so it's a good idea to clean it every now and then (especially after cooking pasta) to ensure no food or residue is blocking the vent.

Don't overfill the pot.

When cooking foods that are prone to foaming, such as beans or pasta, never fill the pot more than half full, and always allow the pressure to naturally release as directed so the foam doesn't spew out of the release vent. For other recipes, don't fill the pot more than two-thirds full.

Don't preheat the pot.

Although some people preheat the Instant Pot or start with very hot water to reduce the overall cooking time, the recipes in this book assume you are using cool water straight from your faucet or refrigerator. Cooking for less time than the recipes call for may result in your food not cooking as intended.

Don't place your pot directly underneath your kitchen cabinets.

In many cases, you'll need to manually release the steam pressure, which will shoot steam from the top of the pot. Be sure that your Instant Pot is situated on a counter with nothing above it so the hot steam doesn't do any damage.

Unplug your machine when you're done using it.

The Instant Pot goes into an automatic Keep Warm mode when the cooking cycle is complete, which is handy when you want to keep your dinner warm. Be sure to unplug the device when you're done using it as a safety precaution.

Now that we've got that covered, here's how to:

Sauté.

The Instant Pot is unique in its ability to also sauté food. This means you can brown meat or sauté vegetables in the pot and then pressure cook in the same pot, or simmer excess liquid out of your sauce when the cooking cycle is over. To use the sauté function, simply press the Sauté button and wait for the beep that tells you the machine is on. Wait 1 to 2 minutes after the beep for the surface to heat up before you add ingredients to the pot, or they may stick to the bottom. (Do not use the lid when using this function; the lid should only be used when pressure cooking.)

Cook on manual.

Press the Manual or Pressure button, depending on your machine, then use the – or + buttons to set the appropriate cooking time. The Manual mode automatically cooks using high pressure, unless you press the Pressure button to switch to low pressure. When pressure cooking, always make sure that the steam release valve is moved to the Sealing position. If your machine doesn't have a Manual setting, it most likely cooks on high pressure automatically.

Make sure the pressure has been reached.

There is a floating valve located on the lid next to the steam release valve that pops up when the pot has come to pressure. It usually takes anywhere from 5 to 20 minutes for the valve to pop up, depending on the recipe, and that's when the cooking cycle will begin counting down. I always keep an eye on my Instant Pot until the floating valve has popped up, to make sure my meal is cooking properly before I walk away. You'll hear steam coming out of the vent shortly before the floating valve pops up.

Quickly release the pressure.

To avoid overcooking, many recipes require that you quickly release the pressure as soon as the Instant Pot has beeped to signal the end of a cooking cycle.

To do that, carefully move the steam release valve to Venting, keeping your hand away from the top of the vent so you don't get burned by the steam. As soon as the floating valve drops, remove the lid to stop the cooking process.

Naturally release the pressure.

Allow the lid to remain on the Instant Pot after the cooking cycle has ended until the specified time has passed. Once the cooking cycle has counted down, the timer will start again, counting *up* the minutes to let you know how long it's been since the cooking cycle stopped. If a recipe requires that you let the pressure naturally release for 10 minutes, don't touch the lid until your Instant Pot reads L0:10, which means it has been on a "keep warm" setting for 10 minutes. When the time has passed, move the steam release valve to the Venting position to release any remaining steam before you remove the lid.

Know that it's safe to remove the lid.

After using a quick or natural release and venting any remaining steam in the pot, the floating valve on the lid, which is next to the steam release valve, will drop, letting you know that all of the pressure has been released. The lid has a safety feature that won't let you open it until the valve has dropped.

Use the pot-in-pot cooking method.

This term refers to cooking two dishes at the same time, using a separate bowl that fits inside the Instant Pot. To use this time-saving method, you'll need a 2.5-inch trivet and a 7-inch oven-safe bowl to hold an extra side dish, like rice or vegetables, that is placed on the trivet over the main entrée, that is cooked directly on the bottom of the Instant Pot. Both the main entrée and the side dish need to cook in a similar amount of time for best results. Check out Korean Chicken Bowls (page 106), Vegetarian Red Beans & Rice (page 138), and Creamy Tuscan Chicken with Mashed "Potatoes" (page 148) for ideas and detailed pot-in-pot instructions. You can also refer to the cooking time charts on page 188 to find items that cook in a similar amount of time if you want to make your own combinations.

Cook for 0 (zero) minutes.

Though it might sound strange, some recipes require that you set the pressure cooking cycle for 0 (zero) minutes to ensure that you don't overcook your ingredients. This cooking cycle simply brings the pot to pressure, which can take anywhere from 5 to 20 minutes, and when it beeps and displays Lo:00 on the screen, you quickly release the pressure by moving the steam release valve to Venting. Releasing the pressure can take 1 to 2 minutes more, so the food will be sufficiently cooked despite the short cooking time.

And if you run into problems, the following tips should help:

I've selected the cooking program, but my pot just says "on." Why hasn't the countdown started yet?

After you select your cooking program and cooking time, the Instant Pot waits 10 seconds to start. When it beeps, you'll see an "On" message as it starts to come to pressure. The cooking cycle won't start counting down until the pot is pressurized, and that process can take anywhere from 5 to 20 minutes after you set the timer, depending on how much liquid is in the pot. The less liquid, the faster it will come to pressure.

How do I adjust the cooking time and pressure setting?

After selecting the Manual or Pressure button, use the – and + buttons to adjust the time. The Manual setting cooks at high pressure automatically, but you can press the Pressure button to adjust the pressure to low on certain models.

Will these recipes work for an 8-quart Instant Pot?

All of these recipes have been successfully tested using the 8-quart Instant Pot Duo. When using this size pot, follow the recipe directions closely, as the 8-quart is prone to displaying "Burn" errors. In any recipe that calls for sautéing meat or vegetables first, always deglaze the pan before bringing the pot to pressure so nothing sticks to the bottom. You can do this by adding a splash of water to the hot pan, then using a wooden spoon or spatula to scrape the bottom of the pan to remove anything that has stuck. Recipes don't always need a full cup of added liquid to make this model come to pressure, but you do need to make sure the ingredients are layered in the correct order to avoid burn errors. Also, keep in mind that vegetables might lose their crunch when cooked in this pot due to the longer pressurization time, particularly in recipes like Eggroll in a Bowl (page 113) and Easy Cauliflower "Rice" (page 56).

Do I need to adjust the cooking time if I double the recipe?

In most cases, you can double a recipe without changing the cooking time, but keep in mind that the increased volume will naturally increase the overall time it takes to prepare the dish because the Instant Pot may take longer to come to pressure. If you're using particularly large cuts of meat, such as large or frozen chicken breasts, they may need a few minutes more to cook. Don't fill your pot more than half full for items that produce foam (like pasta or beans) and more than two-thirds full for everything else.

My Instant Pot never came to pressure. What happened?

If your Instant Pot has been on for more than 25 minutes and the floating valve hasn't popped up to signal that the pressure has been reached, check to make sure you've moved the steam release to Sealing (a common mistake!). If that's not the issue, it could be that the sealing ring in the lid has moved and isn't sealing (see page 15), or that something was stuck to the bottom of your pot, triggering the "Burn" error (see below).

I see a "Burn" error on my Instant Pot. What should I do?

The "Burn" or "Hot" message on the Instant Pot means that the bottom surface of the stainless-steel pot is getting too hot. This can happen when your Instant Pot is empty, when you're heating the pot to sauté something, and when food gets stuck to the bottom of the pot during the cooking process. To remove stuck food, add a splash of water to the hot pan and use a wooden spoon to scrape the bottom until nothing is stuck. The error message will go away quickly and you can continue with your recipe as directed. Also, be sure that you have moved the steam release valve to Sealing so the liquid in your pot doesn't evaporate as it heats up during a pressure cooking cycle.

The floating valve dropped in the middle of a cooking cycle. What should I do?

If steam is coming out of your Instant Pot's floating valve *after* the pressure cooking cycle has started counting down, that means the pot is no longer pressurized and your meal isn't cooking properly. If you can, gently grab the lid by its handle (don't touch the metal as it's very hot) and press down to see if the lid will seal and pop the valve back up. Sometimes that's all it takes. If the valve doesn't pop up, you'll need to press Cancel, move the steam release valve to Venting to make sure the pressure is fully released, and remove the lid. Add a bit more liquid to the pot, starting with just ¼ cup water if it looks like there is plenty of liquid at the bottom, or using more if it looks like much of the cooking liquid has simmered away. Use a wooden spoon to scrape the bottom of the pot, making sure nothing has stuck, then close the lid, move the steam release valve to Sealing, and start the pressure cooking process again. Use your best judgment on the timing based on how much cooking time was left in the cycle when pressure was lost.

Steam is coming out around the rim of my lid. What should I do?

If you see steam coming out around the rim of your lid, and not just from the steam release valve, that is a sign that something is wrong with your sealing ring. You'll have to press Cancel, move the steam release valve to Venting to make sure the pressure is fully released, and remove the lid to check the sealing ring. It's not uncommon for the sealing ring to expand from the heat and move out of place, breaking the seal, so you may be able to fix this issue by pushing the ring back into place and sealing the lid again to continue pressure cooking. If the sealing ring appears to be cracked or damaged, you'll need to buy a replacement.

Why won't my Instant Pot open?

The Instant Pot is designed to stay closed as a safety precaution when the pot is coming to pressure, so you can't open it until the floating valve has dropped. Before attempting to remove the lid, remember to move the steam release valve to Venting and wait for all of the steam to release and the floating valve to drop.

Because I want this book to work for as many models as possible, I've avoided using most specialty settings in these recipes in case your machine doesn't have them. There will always be more than one way to successfully cook an item in the Instant Pot, so the methods in this book are simply one way of doing things that has worked well for me and my recipe testers.

If you have any additional questions regarding your specific model, be sure to check your user manual or reach out directly to the company's customer service line.

Now that we've covered the basics, let's get pressure cooking!

CHAPTER

1

Easy
Breakfasts

Easy-to-Peel Hard-Boiled Eggs

Hard-boiling eggs can be an easy way to get your daily protein, and they make a highly portable snack. Cooking eggs in the Instant Pot ensures perfect results every time: no green ring around the yolk, and as an added bonus, they are amazingly easy to peel!

1. Pour 1 cup water into the Instant Pot and arrange the handled trivet (see page 11) on the bottom. Place the eggs in a single layer on top of the trivet. Secure the lid and move the steam release valve to **Sealing**. Select **Manual/Pressure Cook** to cook on high pressure for 4 minutes for runny yolks or 5 minutes for completely hard-cooked yolks (see the Variation below for medium-cooked eggs).

2. While the eggs are cooking, fill a large bowl with ice and water to create an ice water bath for the eggs.

3. Once the cooking cycle has ended, for runny yolks, immediately move the steam release valve to **Venting** to quickly release the pressure. When the floating valve drops, remove the lid and use tongs to transfer the eggs to the ice water bath to stop the cooking process. (This prevents the green ring around the yolk.) For completely hard-cooked yolks, don't open the lid right away. Let the pressure naturally release for 5 minutes, then move the steam release valve to **Venting** and release the remaining pressure. Transfer the eggs to the ice water bath.

4. Let the eggs cool in the ice water bath for 5 minutes, then peel and serve, or store them in an airtight container in the fridge for 1 week. I find that the eggs are easiest to peel immediately after removing them from the ice water bath, so you may want to peel them all right away, even if you plan on storing some of them in the fridge for later.

VARIATION For medium-cooked eggs (between runny and hard-cooked), cook on high pressure for 3 minutes, then let the pressure naturally release for 3 minutes before venting and opening the lid. Transfer the eggs to the ice water bath to stop the cooking process and let cool for 5 minutes.

Per Egg: Calories 72, Fat 5g, Carbohydrates 0g, Fiber 0g, Protein 6g

MAKES 6

Prep: 4 minutes
Pressurize: 6 minutes
Cook: 5 minutes
Natural Release: 5 minutes
Total: 20 minutes, plus cooling

6 eggs
Ice

Instant Strawberry Jam

MAKES 16 OUNCES

Prep: 5 minutes
Pressurize: 15 minutes
Cook: 6 minutes
Natural Release:
10 minutes
Total: 36 minutes

1 pound frozen
strawberries

¼ cup pure maple syrup
(see page 10)

Pinch of fine sea salt

2 tablespoons chia seeds

Store-bought jams and jellies are often loaded with refined sugar, which can leave you with a sugar crash before it's even time for lunch. Instead, try this naturally sweetened jam to top your morning toast or oatmeal. Using frozen fruit means you get to avoid chopping and peeling, and because the fruit defrosts as the pressure cooker heats up, you don't have to add any additional liquid.

1. Combine the frozen strawberries, maple syrup, and salt in the Instant Pot and secure the lid. Move the steam release valve to **Sealing** and select **Manual/Pressure Cook** to cook at high pressure for 1 minute.

2. When the cooking cycle is complete, let the pressure naturally release for 10 minutes, then move the steam release valve to **Venting** to release any remaining pressure. (This helps you avoid red juice shooting out of the vent.) When the floating valve drops, remove the lid and press **Cancel** to stop the cooking cycle.

3. Press the **Sauté** button and add the chia seeds. Simmer the jam until it begins to thicken, stirring often to make sure it doesn't stick to the bottom of the pan, about 5 minutes.

4. Once the mixture has thickened slightly, or if the jam starts to stick to the pan, press **Cancel** to stop the cooking cycle. Transfer the jam to a 16-ounce glass jar with a lid and store it in the fridge to thicken as it cools. The jam should keep in the fridge for 2 weeks.

Per Tablespoon: Calories 21, Fat 0g, Carbohydrates 4g, Fiber 1g, Protein 0g

Peaches & Cream Steel-Cut Oatmeal

Preparing steel-cut oatmeal on the stove can be time consuming because it requires careful attention and frequent stirring to make sure the oats don't stick to the bottom of your cooking pan. With the Instant Pot, the process is almost completely hands-off. Combine the oats, water, and desired toppings in the pot, set your cooking time, and you're free to accomplish other morning tasks while your oatmeal cooks to perfection. In this version, I use frozen peaches, which are already peeled and chopped, and a touch of cinnamon and coconut milk to create a lightly sweet and creamy breakfast porridge.

1. Combine the steel-cut oats and water in the Instant Pot and give them a stir, then add the peaches, cinnamon, and maple syrup. Secure the lid and move the steam release valve to **Sealing**. Select **Manual/Pressure Cook** to cook on high pressure for 4 minutes.

2. When the cooking cycle has completed, let the pressure naturally release for 15 minutes to finish cooking the oatmeal. (This method prevents the oatmeal from sticking to the bottom of the pot.) Move the steam release valve to **Venting** to release any remaining steam pressure. When the floating valve drops, remove the lid.

3. Stir in the coconut milk, then taste and adjust any seasonings. Serve warm, with additional cinnamon or coconut milk, if desired. Leftover oats can be stored in an airtight container in the fridge for 5 days. You can serve them chilled, or quickly reheat them using the Sauté function of your Instant Pot. (You may need to add a splash of water as you reheat, since oats tend to thicken when chilled.)

NOTE For plain steel-cut oatmeal, I'll often use this method to prepare a large batch of steel-cut oats for the week, which can serve as the base for a number of other toppings, like my Cozy Spiced Fruit (page 31). In this case, cook the steel-cut oats using the timing above, but omit the peaches, cinnamon, maple syrup, and coconut milk. You may want to add up to another 1 cup of water to thin the porridge, as desired, but that can be added after cooking, so that it doesn't increase the pressurize time.

Per Serving: Calories 340, Fat 5g, Carbohydrates 65g, Fiber 8g, Protein 10g

SERVES 4

Prep: 5 minutes
Pressurize: 10 minutes
Cook: 4 minutes
Natural Release: 15 minutes
Total: 34 minutes

2 cups steel-cut oats

4 cups water

1 pound frozen sliced peaches

½ teaspoon ground cinnamon, plus more for serving (optional)

¼ cup pure maple syrup (see page 10)

½ cup full-fat coconut milk (see page 8), plus more for serving (optional)

Peanut Butter Crunch Granola Bars

MAKES 10

Prep: 5 minutes
Pressurize: 5 minutes
Cook: 20 minutes
Natural Release:
10 minutes
Total: 40 minutes,
plus cooling

1 cup quick-cooking oats
(see Note)

⅓ cup pure maple syrup
(see page 10)

½ cup all-natural peanut
butter

1 tablespoon extra-virgin
olive oil

¼ teaspoon fine sea salt

⅓ cup dried cranberries
or raisins

½ cup raw pumpkin seeds
(pepitas)

These gluten-free and naturally sweetened granola bars are the perfect snack to keep stashed in your fridge or take on the go. They are easily adapted to any ingredients you have on hand, so go crazy with the add-ins. Be sure to use a brand of peanut butter, or other nut or seed butter, that has no added oil or sugar for the healthiest results.

1. Line a 7-inch round pan with parchment paper.

2. In a large bowl, combine the oats, maple syrup, peanut butter, olive oil, and salt and stir well. Fold in the dried fruit and pumpkin seeds, then pour the batter into the prepared pan, using a spatula to press the mixture evenly into the bottom of the pan.

3. Pour 1 cup water into the Instant Pot and arrange the handled trivet (see page 11) on the bottom. Place the pan on top of the trivet. Cover the pan with an upside-down plate or another piece of parchment to protect the granola bars from condensation. Secure the lid, moving the steam release valve to **Sealing**. Select **Manual/Pressure Cook** to cook on high pressure for 20 minutes.

4. Let the pressure naturally release for 10 minutes, then move the steam release valve to **Venting**. When the floating valve drops, remove the lid. Use oven mitts to lift the trivet and the pan out of the pot. Let the granola cool completely in the pan, at least 1 hour.

5. Cut the cooled granola into 10 pieces. The round pan will make the bars uneven in size, but you can cut them into uniform wedges if you'd prefer. Wrap them individually in plastic wrap or place them in an airtight container and store in the fridge for 2 weeks.

NOTE Don't be tempted to use old-fashioned oats instead of quick-cooking oats in this recipe. The bars will not hold together as well, and the texture won't be as appealing. Because oats can be exposed to cross-contamination when processed, be sure to look for certified gluten-free oats, if needed.

Per Serving: Calories 194, Fat 11g, Carbohydrates 20g, Fiber 2g, Protein 6g

Cozy Spiced Fruit

This warm fruit topping is a holiday staple in my home. My mom used to make it with canned fruit, lots of sugar, and a hint of curry powder, which may sound strange but is surprisingly delicious. Using mostly frozen fruit cuts down on chopping time and eliminates the need for extra water. As the fruit thaws it provides plenty of liquid to bring the pot to pressure. Maple syrup adds the perfect amount of natural sweetness to balance out the spice. Serve this with a bowl of steel-cut oatmeal or over a stack of pancakes for a warm and comforting way to start your day.

1. Combine the peaches, pineapple, cherries, pears, maple syrup, and curry powder in the Instant Pot and secure the lid. Move the steam release valve to **Sealing** and select **Manual/Pressure Cook** to cook on high pressure for 1 minute.

2. When the cooking cycle is complete, quickly move the steam release valve to **Venting** to release the steam pressure. When the floating valve drops, remove the lid and stir the mixture well, adding more curry powder if you like it spicy.

3. Serve the fruit warm, either as a side dish or as a topping for oatmeal. It is normal for the fruit to be sitting in its juices when this dish is done. Scoop it with a slotted spoon and let the juices drain back into the pot before serving. Store leftovers in an airtight container in the fridge for 5 days.

Per Serving: Calories 145, Fat 1g, Carbohydrates 37g, Fiber 4g, Protein 1g

SERVES 6

Prep: 5 minutes
Pressurize: 10 minutes
Cook: 1 minute
Quick Release
Total: 16 minutes

1 pound sliced frozen peaches

1 pound frozen pineapple chunks

1 cup frozen and pitted dark sweet cherries

2 ripe pears, sliced

¼ cup pure maple syrup (see page 10)

1 teaspoon curry powder, plus more as needed

Steel-cut oatmeal (see Note, page 27), for serving (optional)

Maple-Cinnamon Cereal Bowls

SERVES 6

Prep: 5 minutes,
plus soaking
Pressurize: 9 minutes
Cook: 1 minute
Natural Release:
10 minutes
Total: 25 minutes

2 cups buckwheat groats,
soaked for at least
20 minutes and up to
overnight

3 cups water

1 teaspoon ground
cinnamon

¼ cup pure maple syrup
(see page 10)

1 teaspoon vanilla extract

¼ teaspoon fine sea salt

Almond milk, for serving

Chopped or sliced fresh
fruit, for serving

If a bowl of cereal doesn't keep you full until lunch, try these heartier whole-grain cereal bowls. They're made with buckwheat groats, which despite its name is not at all related to wheat and is naturally gluten-free. I like to make a big batch of this cereal at the beginning of the week, store it in individual serving containers, and then eat it like I would cereal for a fast and satisfying breakfast. It's delicious hot or cold. Soaking buckwheat in a bowl of water for as little as 20 minutes before cooking will help remove its natural bitterness. You can also soak it overnight in the fridge.

1. Drain and rinse the buckwheat, then combine it with the water, cinnamon, maple syrup, vanilla, and salt in the Instant Pot and secure the lid. Move the steam release valve to **Sealing** and select **Manual/Pressure Cook** to cook on high pressure for 1 minute.

2. Let the pressure naturally release for 10 minutes before moving the steam release valve to **Venting**. When the floating valve drops, carefully remove the lid and stir the cooked grains.

3. Serve the buckwheat right away with almond milk and fresh fruit, or store about 1 cup of cooked grains in each of several airtight containers in the fridge for 1 week and serve chilled or warm for a quick weekday breakfast.

VARIATION To use a different whole grain in these cereal bowls, refer to the chart on page 189 for proper cooking times.

Per Serving: Calories 235, Fat 2g, Carbohydrates 52g, Fiber 6g, Protein 7g

Take-Along Veggie Frittatas

These portable veggie frittatas are the perfect protein-packed breakfast if you need to eat on the go. I cook them in 8-ounce widemouthed glass jars for easy travel, storage, and portion control, but you could also prepare this in a 7-inch round pan (see Variation, below) to make a larger frittata served by the slice. Feel free to swap out the veggies to use up anything you have on hand. The flavor combinations are limitless.

1. Combine the eggs, salt, bell pepper, green onions, spinach, feta, and a few grinds of black pepper in a mixing bowl and stir well.

2. Grease four 8-ounce mason jars with olive oil and then divide the mixture evenly among the jars.

3. Pour 1 cup water into the Instant Pot and arrange the handled trivet (see page 11) on the bottom. Place the four jars in a single layer on the trivet and secure the lid. Move the steam release valve to **Sealing** and select **Manual/Pressure Cook** to cook on high pressure for 8 minutes. Let the pressure naturally release for 10 minutes, then move the steam release valve to **Venting** to release any remaining steam. When the floating valve drops, remove the lid.

4. Use oven mitts to remove the jars. Tip the frittatas out of the jars and onto plates to serve warm, or cover the jars and store in the fridge for 5 days. Enjoy these frittatas chilled or reheat them, if desired.

VARIATION To bake this as a single large frittata, grease a 7-inch round pan with olive oil and pour in the mixture. Follow the given instructions, but cook on high pressure for 10 minutes, then let the pressure naturally release for 10 minutes before removing the lid.

Per Serving: Calories 157, Fat 7g, Carbohydrates 5g, Fiber 2g, Protein 16g

SERVES 4

Prep: 10 minutes
Pressurize: 10 minutes
Cook: 8 minutes
Natural Release: 10 minutes
Total: 38 minutes

6 eggs

½ teaspoon fine sea salt

1 red bell pepper, seeded and chopped

3 green onions, tender white and green parts only, chopped

1 cup chopped spinach

¼ cup crumbled feta cheese

Freshly ground black pepper

Flourless Banana Oat Cake

SERVES 6 TO 8

Prep: 10 minutes
Pressurize: 5 minutes
Cook: 40 minutes
Natural Release:
10 minutes
Total: 1 hour 5 minutes,
plus cooling

½ cup mashed ripe
banana (1 large banana)

½ cup almond butter

½ cup coconut sugar

2 eggs

½ teaspoon baking soda

½ teaspoon cinnamon

¼ teaspoon fine sea salt

1 cup quick-cooking oats
(see Note)

This flourless breakfast cake is like a cross between baked oatmeal and banana bread. It has a hearty chew and texture from the oats, and it won't spike your blood sugar the way a traditional banana bread might because it's naturally sweetened. The riper your banana, the sweeter the cake will be, so be sure to use a banana with lots of black spots on the skin for the best results.

1. Line a 7-inch round pan with a piece of parchment paper and set it aside.

2. In a large bowl, combine the banana, almond butter, coconut sugar, eggs, baking soda, cinnamon, and salt. Stir well to break up any lumps, then stir in the oats. Pour the batter into the prepared pan and use a spatula to even out the top.

3. Pour 1 cup water into the Instant Pot and arrange the handled trivet (see page 11) on the bottom. Place the pan on top of the trivet. To protect the cake from condensation, cover it with an upside-down plate or another piece of parchment paper.

4. Secure the lid and move the pressure valve to **Sealing**. Select **Manual/Pressure Cook** to cook on high pressure for 40 minutes, then let the pressure naturally release for 10 minutes. Move the steam release valve to **Venting** to release any remaining steam. When the floating valve drops, remove the lid.

5. Use oven mitts to lift the trivet and the pan out of the pot. Let the cake cool completely in the pan to firm up, about 30 minutes, then remove the cake from the pan. Slice and serve at room temperature or chilled. Store leftovers in an airtight container in the fridge for 1 week.

MAKE IT VEGAN Omit the eggs and add 2 tablespoons ground flax or chia seeds, 3 tablespoons water, and 1 teaspoon raw apple cider vinegar. The resulting cake will be slightly more fragile, but still delicious.

NOTE Don't be tempted to use old-fashioned oats instead of quick-cooking oats in this recipe, as the texture won't be as appealing. Because oats can be exposed to cross-contamination when processed, be sure to look for certified gluten-free oats, if needed.

Per Serving: Calories 220, Fat 11g, Carbohydrates 26g, Fiber 4g, Protein 7g

Italian-Style Shakshuka

Shakshuka is a popular Middle Eastern breakfast dish featuring eggs cooked in a savory tomato sauce. In this recipe, I've given it an Italian flare by using store-bought marinara sauce (with no added sugar), so you don't have to make tomato sauce from scratch on a busy morning. I've also thrown in some kale for added nutrition. Serve this on its own in a bowl, or with whole-grain toast.

1. Press **Sauté** and add the olive oil to the Instant Pot. Once the oil is hot but not smoking, add the onion, garlic, and a pinch of salt and sauté until softened, about 5 minutes. Add the water, marinara sauce, and kale and stir well with a wooden spoon, scraping the bottom of the pot to make sure nothing sticks.

2. Press **Cancel**. Use the spoon to make four small wells evenly spaced in the marinara sauce, then carefully crack an egg into each well. Season the eggs with salt and pepper.

3. Secure the lid and move the steam release valve to **Sealing**. Select **Manual/Pressure Cook** to cook on high pressure for 0 minutes (see page 17). When the pot has come to pressure and the screen reads L0:00, quickly release the pressure by immediately moving the steam release valve to **Venting**. (This method of cooking produces a hard-cooked yolk when using an 8-quart pot, and a slightly softer hard-cooked yolk when using a 6-quart pot. If you prefer runny eggs, you might want to cook them on the stove instead.)

4. When the floating valve drops, remove the lid and use a slotted spoon to scoop the eggs, sauce, and plenty of the cooked veggies into a small serving dish. Top with cheese and chopped parsley and serve immediately as is, or with a few slices of toast.

MAKE IT VEGAN Omit the eggs and cheese, and use cooked chickpeas as a plant-based source of protein, instead. Because the chickpeas are already cooked, you can use the 0-minute pressure cooking cycle noted above.

Per Serving: Calories 182, Fat 11g, Carbohydrates 12g, Fiber 3g, Protein 11g

SERVES 4

Prep: 10 minutes
Pressurize: 5 minutes
Cook: 5 minutes
Quick Release
Total: 20 minutes

1 tablespoon extra-virgin olive oil

½ yellow onion, chopped

2 cloves garlic, minced

Fine sea salt

¼ cup water

2½ cups marinara sauce

1 cup chopped kale, stems removed

4 eggs

Freshly ground black pepper

Crumbled feta or grated Parmesan cheese, for garnish (optional)

Chopped fresh flat-leaf parsley or basil, for garnish (optional)

Toast slices, for serving (optional)

Asparagus & Leek Frittata

SERVES 4

Prep: 10 minutes
Pressurize: 6 minutes
Cook: 10 minutes
Natural Release:
10 minutes
Total: 36 minutes,
plus cooling

6 eggs

¼ teaspoon fine sea salt

Freshly ground black
pepper

8 ounces asparagus
spears, woody stems
removed, cut into
1-inch pieces

1 cup thinly sliced leeks

¼ cup grated Parmesan
cheese

Chopped green onions,
for garnish

Fresh flat-leaf parsley,
for garnish

Frittatas are easy to customize with whatever vegetables are in season, so just use my suggestions here as a jumping-off point. Traditional recipes often require you to first cook the frittata over the stove and then finish it off in your oven's broiler, but this method streamlines the process to make it as hands-off as possible.

1. Grease a 7-inch round pan generously with olive oil to prevent sticking. In a large mixing bowl, combine the eggs, salt, and several grinds of black pepper and beat well with a fork. Fold in the asparagus, leeks, and Parmesan and pour the mixture into the prepared pan.

2. Pour 1 cup water into the Instant Pot and arrange the handled trivet (see page 11) on the bottom. Place the pan on top of the trivet. Secure the lid and move the steam release valve to **Sealing**. Select **Manual/Pressure Cook** to cook on high pressure for 10 minutes. Let the pressure naturally release for 10 minutes, then move the steam release valve to **Venting** to release any remaining pressure. When the floating valve drops, remove the lid.

3. Use oven mitts to lift the trivet and the pan out of the pot. Let the frittata cool for 5 minutes in the pan before cutting and serving. Store leftovers in an airtight container in the fridge for 5 days.

Per Serving: Calories 232, Fat 14g, Carbohydrates 5g, Fiber 1g, Protein 19g

Huevos Rancheros

Huevos rancheros is a filling breakfast that combines savory Mexican ingredients with protein-rich eggs. Using prepared salsa as the liquid in this recipe creates plenty of flavor with minimal effort. Mild, medium, or hot—go as spicy as you like! Serve this over your favorite tortillas, in lettuce wraps, or on a bed of greens for a satisfying and comforting meal.

1. Press the **Sauté** button and add the olive oil to the Instant Pot. Once the oil is hot but not smoking, add the onion and bell pepper and sauté until tender, about 6 minutes. Press **Cancel**, then stir in the cumin and cayenne with a wooden spoon or spatula while the pot is still hot.

2. Add the beans, salsa, and water to the pot and stir well, scraping the bottom to make sure nothing sticks. Carefully crack the eggs into the salsa, keeping them spaced at least 1 inch apart. Sprinkle salt and black pepper on top of each egg.

3. Secure the lid and move the steam release valve to **Sealing**. Select **Manual/ Pressure Cook** and cook on high pressure for 0 minutes (see page 17). When the pot has come to pressure and the screen reads LO:00, quickly release the pressure by immediately moving the steam release valve to **Venting**. (This method of cooking produces a hard-cooked yolk when using an 8-quart pot, and a slightly softer hard-cooked yolk when using a 6-quart pot. If you prefer runny eggs, you might want to cook them on the stove instead.)

4. When the floating valve drops, remove the lid and use a slotted spoon to scoop the eggs and some of the salsa mixture onto a tortilla. Top with additional salsa and the garnishes of your choice, and serve immediately.

MAKE IT VEGAN Omit the eggs and use sweet potato instead. Cut a medium sweet potato into 1-inch pieces and cook them in the salsa at high pressure for 5 minutes, then quickly release the pressure to vent and remove the lid.

Per Serving: Calories 242, Fat 9g, Carbohydrates 27g, Fiber 9g, Protein 12g

SERVES 6

Prep: 5 minutes
Pressurize: 6 minutes
Cook: 6 minutes
Quick Release
Total: 17 minutes

1 tablespoon extra-virgin olive oil

½ red onion, chopped

1 green bell pepper, seeded and chopped

1 teaspoon ground cumin

⅛ teaspoon cayenne pepper (optional)

1½ cups cooked black beans, or one 15-ounce can black beans, drained and rinsed

1½ cups prepared salsa, plus more for serving

½ cup water

6 eggs

Fine sea salt and freshly ground black pepper

6 corn tortillas

Chopped green onions, crumbled feta cheese, sliced avocado, and chopped fresh cilantro, for garnish (optional)

CHAPTER

2

Healthy
Side Dishes

Cinnamon Applesauce

Applesauce is a heathy and convenient snack to have on hand, but many store-bought varieties include added sugar and unwanted preservatives. Luckily, it's incredibly easy to make applesauce in the Instant Pot. It's naturally sweet and delicious on its own, but you can add additional flavors to keep things interesting.

1. Add the apples, cinnamon, and water to the Instant Pot and secure the lid. Move the steam release valve to **Sealing** and select **Manual/Pressure Cook** to cook on high pressure for 10 minutes.

2. Let the pressure naturally release for 10 minutes, then move the steam release valve to **Venting**. When the floating valve drops, remove the lid.

3. Use a potato masher or immersion blender to puree the apples to the consistency of your choice. Serve the applesauce warm, or transfer it to an airtight container and chill in the fridge until ready to serve. Store the applesauce in the fridge for 1 week or in the freezer for 3 months.

VARIATION For an extra-fruity applesauce, omit the cinnamon and add 1 pound of frozen fruit, such as mangoes or strawberries, to the pot. Feel free to get creative, as the cooking time doesn't change with any of these additions. (It may take a few more minutes to come to pressure, however.)

Per ½ Cup: Calories 65, Fat 0g, Carbohydrates 17g, Fiber 3g, Protein 1g

MAKES 6 CUPS

Prep: 10 minutes
Pressurize: 5 minutes
Cook: 10 minutes
Natural Release: 10 minutes
Total: 35 minutes

3 pounds apples (such as Fuji or McIntosh), peeled and sliced

½ teaspoon ground cinnamon

½ cup water

Healthy Hummus

MAKES 2½ CUPS

Prep: 5 minutes
Pressurize: 15 minutes
Cook: 50 minutes
Natural Release:
20 minutes
Total: 1 hour 30 minutes

1 cup dried chickpeas
(not soaked; see Note)

3½ cups water

¼ cup tahini

2 tablespoons freshly
squeezed lemon juice

2 cloves garlic, minced

1 teaspoon fine sea salt

1 teaspoon ground cumin

Freshly ground black
pepper

Making hummus from scratch is incredibly easy with an Instant Pot. If you have trouble digesting beans, soak the chickpeas ahead of time. I'm often in such a rush that I don't soak them at all, and I don't notice the difference. This recipe is an affordable alternative to store-bought hummus, and is significantly lower in fat and calories, too. Enjoy it with your favorite sliced veggies for a quick and satisfying snack, or as a spread on a sandwich or wrap.

1. Place the dried chickpeas in the Instant Pot and add 3 cups of the water. Secure the lid and move the steam release valve to **Sealing**. Select **Manual/Pressure Cook** to cook on high pressure for 50 minutes.

2. Let the pressure naturally release for 20 minutes, then move the steam release valve to **Venting**. When the floating valve drops, remove the lid and drain the cooked chickpeas in a colander.

3. To blend the hummus, you can either return the cooked chickpeas to the Instant Pot and use an immersion blender, or add the chickpeas to a food processor or blender. Add the tahini, the remaining ½ cup water, the lemon juice, garlic, salt, cumin, and several grinds of black pepper and blend until smooth. Adjust the seasonings to your taste. Serve the hummus right away or store it in an airtight container in the fridge for 1 week.

NOTE To ease digestion, soak the dried chickpeas in water for up to 10 hours in the fridge. Drain and rinse the chickpeas in a colander, then cook them at high pressure for 12 minutes. Let the pressure release naturally, as directed above.

Per ¼ Cup: Calories 82, Fat 4g, Carbohydrates 13g, Fiber 6g, Protein 4g

Sesame Green Beans

This easy side dish is one of my favorite ways to serve green beans. The Instant Pot steams them in a manner of minutes and then you use the sauté function to cook the beans in a spicy garlic sesame oil. As simple as it sounds, the flavor is addictive, and I love that the green beans still retain a slight crunch.

1. Pour 1 cup water into the Instant Pot and arrange a steamer basket on the bottom. Add the green beans to the basket, making sure the beans don't touch the water. Secure the lid and move the steam release valve to **Sealing**. Select **Manual/Pressure Cook** and cook at high pressure for 0 minutes (see page 17).

2. When the pot beeps and the screen reads L0:00, quickly release the pressure by moving the steam release valve to **Venting**. When the floating valve drops, remove the lid and press **Cancel** to stop the cooking cycle. Use oven mitts to remove the steamer basket full of beans and set them aside. Drain the water from the pot.

3. Press **Sauté** and add the olive oil to the Instant Pot. Once the oil is hot but not smoking, add the garlic, sesame oil, and red pepper flakes. Stir briefly, about 30 seconds, then add the steamed green beans and stir well to coat the beans in the fragrant oil, about 30 seconds more.

4. Season with salt to taste (I use ½ teaspoon), and serve warm with a sprinkling of sesame seeds on top. Store leftovers in an airtight container in the fridge for 5 days; they make a great chilled topping for salads.

Per Serving: Calories 102, Fat 7g, Carbohydrates 9g, Fiber 4g, Protein 3g

SERVES 4

Prep: 5 minutes
Pressurize: 6 minutes
Cook: 1 minute
Quick Release
Total: 12 minutes

1 pound green beans, trimmed and cut into 1-inch pieces

1 tablespoon extra-virgin olive oil

2 cloves garlic, minced

1½ teaspoons toasted sesame oil

¼ teaspoon red pepper flakes

Fine sea salt

1 tablespoon sesame seeds

Not-Fried Pinto Beans

SERVES 4

Prep: 10 minutes,
plus soaking
Pressurize: 12 minutes
Cook: 20 minutes
Natural Release:
10 minutes
Total: 52 minutes

1 cup dried pinto beans,
soaked for 8 hours and
drained (see page 68)

3 cups water

½ yellow onion, chopped

2 cloves garlic, minced

1 teaspoon ground cumin

1 teaspoon chili powder

¼ teaspoon freshly
ground black pepper

Pinch of cayenne pepper
(optional)

½ to ¾ teaspoon fine
sea salt

Chopped fresh cilantro,
for garnish

Lime wedges, for garnish

If you love the flavor of refried beans but would rather avoid the lard they
are typically cooked in, you'll love this fat-free version. Instead of cooking
the beans twice, as you would with traditional refried beans, you simply cook
pinto beans until tender and then mash them until creamy. These make a
flavorful and filling side dish. If you enjoy leftovers, double the recipe so you
can use them in burritos or tacos later in the week.

1. Combine the drained beans, water, onion, and garlic in the Instant Pot. Stir
   well, making sure the beans are submerged. Secure the lid and move the
   steam release valve to **Sealing**. Select **Manual/Pressure Cook** to cook at high
   pressure for 20 minutes.

2. When the cooking cycle is complete, let the pressure naturally release for
   10 minutes, then move the steam release valve to **Venting** to release any
   remaining pressure. When the floating valve drops, remove the lid and drain
   the beans, reserving the liquid. Return the cooked beans to the Instant Pot,
   and stir in ½ cup of the reserved cooking liquid, along with the cumin, chili
   powder, black pepper, cayenne, and ½ teaspoon salt. Use a potato masher to
   mash the cooked beans until smooth, leaving some texture if you like. (You
   can use an immersion blender for pureed beans, if you prefer.)

3. Taste and adjust the seasoning, adding more salt as needed, and serve warm
   with a garnish of cilantro and a squeeze of lime juice. Store leftover beans in
   an airtight container in the fridge for 1 week.

Per Serving: Calories 74, Fat 0g, Carbohydrates 14g, Fiber 5g, Protein 4g

Lightened-Up Mashed Potatoes & Gravy

Potatoes are rich in vitamins and minerals, like vitamin C and potassium, but when you load them up with butter and sour cream, unfortunately they can't be considered a health food. In this lightened-up version, I skip the butter and mix in nutrient-rich cauliflower to lower the overall carbohydrate content. Top them with a flavorful vegetable-based gravy, which you can make at the same time in your Instant Pot, for a surprisingly low-fat side dish.

1. Cut the potatoes into 1-inch chunks, reserving one cut-up potato for the gravy.

2. Combine the onion, mushrooms, the reserved cut-up potato, the garlic, soy sauce, ¼ teaspoon salt, several grinds of black pepper, and the water in the Instant Pot. Arrange a steamer basket on top of the mushroom mixture, and place the cauliflower florets and the remaining potatoes into the basket. Secure the lid and move the steam release valve to **Sealing**. Select **Manual/Pressure Cook** to cook on high pressure for 10 minutes.

3. When the cooking cycle is complete, let the pressure naturally release for 10 minutes, then move the steam release valve to **Venting** to release any remaining pressure. When the floating valve drops, remove the lid.

4. Use oven mitts to remove the steamer basket and transfer the cauliflower and potatoes to a large bowl. Use a potato masher to mash them, then season generously with salt and pepper to taste. (Add a little more water if you want a thinner consistency.) Stir in the chives.

5. Use an immersion blender to blend the gravy directly in the bottom of the Instant Pot. Alternatively, you can pour the mixture into a blender and blend until smooth. Taste and adjust the seasonings.

6. Serve the mash immediately with the gravy on top. Store leftovers in an airtight container in the fridge for 5 days.

VARIATION For a really low-carb dish, swap some of the potatoes for an equal amount of cauliflower to make mashed cauliflower "potatoes."

MAKE IT GLUTEN-FREE Use tamari instead of soy sauce.

Per Serving: Calories 168, Fat 0g, Carbohydrates 50g, Fiber 6g, Protein 6g

SERVES 6

Prep: 10 minutes
Pressurize: 8 minutes
Cook: 10 minutes
Natural Release: 10 minutes
Total: 38 minutes

2 pounds Yukon gold potatoes

1 yellow onion, chopped

4 ounces cremini mushrooms, chopped (about 1 cup)

2 cloves garlic, minced

2 tablespoons soy sauce or tamari

Fine sea salt and freshly ground black pepper

1 cup water

1 pound cauliflower, cut into florets

2 tablespoons chopped fresh chives

Easy Cauliflower "Rice"

SERVES 4

Prep: 5 minutes
Pressurize: 5 minutes
Cook: 1 minute
Quick Release
Total: 11 minutes

1 head cauliflower, cut into florets

Fine sea salt

Cauliflower "rice" is one of my favorite low-carb sides because it's neutral in flavor and can be served with any number of dishes as a substitute for white rice. Normally, you use a food processor or box grater to rice the cauliflower while it's raw, but with the Instant Pot, you can use a potato masher to break up the cauliflower directly in the pot for a faster preparation.

1. Pour 1 cup water into the Instant Pot and arrange a steamer basket on the bottom. Place the cauliflower florets into the steamer basket, making sure that none of the cauliflower touches the water.

2. Secure the lid and move the steam release valve to **Sealing**. Select **Manual/ Pressure Cook** to cook on high pressure for 1 minute. When the cooking cycle is complete, immediately move the steam release valve to **Venting** to quickly release the steam pressure. This ensures the cauliflower doesn't overcook. When the floating valve drops, press **Cancel** and remove the lid.

3. Use oven mitts to lift the steam basket out of the pot and pour out any water from the pot. Add the cooked cauliflower back to the pot. Season generously with salt and use a potato masher to break up the cauliflower into a ricelike consistency. Serve warm. Store leftovers in an airtight container in the fridge for 5 days.

LOW-CARB TIP When pot-in-pot cooking (see page 16), you can swap the white rice and its cooking water in a recipe with a bowl of cauliflower florets instead. Cauliflower can withstand up to 12 minutes of pressure cooking in a raised bowl on a trivet, and is then easily broken up into ricelike pieces with a fork. The "rice" is a little softer than the method above, but it doesn't get much easier or faster! Try it with Korean Chicken Bowls (page 106) or Kung Pao Chickpeas (page 125).

Per Serving: Calories 57, Fat 0g, Carbohydrates 12g, Fiber 6g, Protein 4g

Savory Mashed Sweet Potatoes

Instead of topping baked sweet potatoes with marshmallows at holiday gatherings, I prefer to serve these nutrient-rich spuds with a savory twist. The Instant Pot helps speed the cooking process, steaming the sweet potatoes in just 8 minutes, then you mash them in the same pot for easy cleanup.

1. Pour 1 cup water into the Instant Pot and arrange a steamer basket on the bottom. Place the sweet potatoes in the basket, making sure the potatoes don't touch the water. Secure the lid and move the steam release valve to **Sealing**. Select **Manual/Pressure Cook** to cook on high pressure for 8 minutes.

2. When the cooking cycle is complete, quickly release the pressure by moving the steam release valve to **Venting**. When the floating valve drops, remove the lid and press **Cancel** to stop the cooking cycle. Use oven mitts to lift out the steam basket and pour the water out of the pot.

3. Pour the drained sweet potatoes back into the pot and use a potato masher to mash the potatoes. Add the thyme, rosemary, olive oil, salt, and several grinds of pepper and stir well to combine. Taste and adjust the seasonings, then serve warm. Store leftovers in an airtight container in the fridge for 5 days.

SERVES 4

Prep: 9 minutes
Pressurize: 6 minutes
Cook: 8 minutes
Quick Release
Total: 23 minutes

2 pounds sweet potatoes, peeled and cut into 1-inch chunks

1 teaspoon minced fresh thyme

½ teaspoon minced fresh rosemary

1 tablespoon extra-virgin olive oil (optional)

½ teaspoon fine sea salt

Freshly ground black pepper

Per Serving: Calories 224, Fat 4g, Carbohydrates 46g, Fiber 7g, Protein 4g

Garlic-Parmesan Spaghetti Squash

SERVES 4

Prep: 5 minutes
Pressurize: 5 minutes
Cook: 10 minutes
Quick Release
Total: 20 minutes

One 3-pound spaghetti squash

1 tablespoon extra-virgin olive oil

3 cloves garlic, minced

1 teaspoon fine sea salt

Freshly ground black pepper

¼ cup grated Parmesan cheese

Chopped fresh flat-leaf parsley, for garnish

Spaghetti squash is one of my favorite low-carb noodle alternatives because you don't need a spiralizer or any other special equipment to create the noodlelike strands. You can cook the spaghetti squash whole (see One-Pot Turkey Bolognese, page 144), but scooping out the seeds is a lot easier when you cut the squash in half before cooking. This has become my go-to method for cooking spaghetti squash, as the Instant Pot cooks it in just a fraction of the time it would take in an oven.

1. Pour 1 cup water into the Instant Pot and arrange the handled trivet (see page 11) on the bottom. Cut the spaghetti squash in half crosswise (for longer spaghetti strands) and use a spoon to scoop out and discard the seeds. Place the two cut halves on the Instant Pot trivet (they may have to face each other to fit in the pot as if the squash were still whole) and secure the lid.

2. Move the steam release valve to **Sealing** and select **Manual/Pressure Cook** to cook on high pressure for 7 minutes. When the cooking cycle is complete, immediately move the steam release valve to **Venting** to quickly release any remaining steam pressure. When the floating valve drops, remove the lid and press **Cancel** to stop the cooking cycle.

3. Use oven mitts to transfer the squash halves to a cutting board. Remove the trivet and drain the water from the pot, then dry the pot and return it to the Instant Pot housing.

4. Press **Sauté** and add the olive oil to the pot. Once the oil is hot but not smoking, add the garlic and stir just until fragrant, about 30 seconds.

5. Hold one half of the spaghetti squash with an oven mitt and use a fork to scrape the cooked squash out of the shell directly into the pot. Repeat with the other squash half, then stir in the salt and several grinds of pepper. Stir in the Parmesan cheese. Taste and adjust the seasonings as needed, then serve warm with a sprinkling of parsley. Store leftovers in an airtight container in the fridge for 5 days.

MAKE IT VEGAN Omit the Parmesan and season with 2 to 3 tablespoons nutritional yeast, to taste.

Per Serving: Calories 158, Fat 11g, Carbohydrates 5g, Fiber 1g, Protein 10g

Instant Vegetable Medley

Steamed vegetables are one of the easiest and healthiest things you can make in the Instant Pot, and I like to boost their flavor by sautéing them in garlic and olive oil just before serving. Adding a touch of healthy fat to this side dish helps the body absorb their important fat-soluble vitamins, like vitamins A, D, E, and K. Vegetables can overcook if you don't quickly release the pressure, so stay close to your Instant Pot or you may wind up with mushy vegetables.

SERVES 4

Prep: 5 minutes
Pressurize: 1 minute
Cook: 1 minute
Quick Release
Total: 12 minutes

1 pound assorted non-starchy vegetables, such as cauliflower, carrots, and green beans

2 tablespoons extra-virgin olive oil

1 clove garlic, minced

Fine sea salt and freshly ground black pepper

Chopped fresh parsley, for garnish

1. Pour 1 cup water into the Instant Pot and arrange a steamer basket on the bottom. Place the vegetables in the steamer basket, making sure the vegetables aren't touching the water. Secure the lid and move the steam release valve to **Sealing**. Select **Manual/Pressure Cook** to cook on high pressure for 0 minutes (see page 17).

2. When the pot beeps and the screen reads L0:00, immediately move the steam release valve to **Venting** to quickly release the steam pressure. When the floating valve drops, remove the lid and press **Cancel** to stop the cooking cycle. The vegetables should be tender, but with some tooth to them. Use oven mitts to remove the steamer basket full of vegetables, drain the water from the pot, then dry the pot and return it to the Instant Pot housing.

3. Press **Sauté** and add the olive oil to the Instant Pot. Once the oil is hot but not smoking, add in the garlic and stir briefly, just until fragrant, about 30 seconds. Add the steamed vegetables to the pot and stir well to coat them in the garlic-infused olive oil, about 30 seconds more.

4. Season generously with salt and pepper, then serve warm with parsley on top. Store leftover vegetables in an airtight container in the fridge for 1 week. They make for great toppings in a salad or grain bowl.

VARIATIONS To use frozen vegetables, follow the instructions as given. The vegetables will defrost and heat while the pot is coming to pressure, though they will be slightly softer than using fresh. For cooking starchy vegetables, such as potatoes, parsnips, or winter squash, cut them into 1-inch pieces and steam for 4 minutes to become tender.

Per Serving: Calories 104, Fat 4g, Carbohydrates 10g, Fiber 3g, Protein 2g

Fresh Bulgur Pilaf

SERVES 4

Prep: 10 minutes
Pressurize: 6 minutes
Cook: 7 minutes
Natural Release:
15 minutes
Total: 38 minutes

1 tablespoon extra-virgin olive oil

½ red onion, diced

1 clove garlic, minced

1 teaspoon minced fresh ginger (about ½-inch knob)

½ teaspoon turmeric

½ teaspoon ground cumin

1 cup bulgur

1¼ cups water

½ teaspoon fine sea salt

½ cup finely diced celery

¼ cup loosely packed chopped fresh mint

¼ cup loosely packed chopped fresh flat-leaf parsley

2 tablespoons freshly squeezed lemon juice

½ cup finely chopped walnuts

½ cup golden raisins

Bulgur is a quick-cooking grain made from wheat, and is high in minerals such as magnesium and iron. For a light and refreshing dish, I like to pair it with vegetables and herbs, like mint and parsley, but you could swap in fresh dill, basil, or cilantro to mimic the seasonings in your main entrée if you like. I stir in raw celery at the end for added crunch, but if you prefer the celery to be tender, cook it with the bulgur instead.

1. Press **Sauté** and add the olive oil to the Instant Pot. Once the oil is hot but not smoking, add the onion and sauté until softened, about 5 minutes. Add the garlic, ginger, turmeric, and cumin and stir with a wooden spoon or spatula for 1 minute.

2. Press **Cancel**, then add the bulgur, water, and salt. Stir well, scraping the bottom of the pot to make sure nothing sticks. Secure the lid and move the steam release valve to **Sealing**. Select **Manual/Pressure Cook** to cook on high pressure for 1 minute.

3. When the cooking cycle is complete, let the pressure naturally release for 15 minutes. Move the steam release valve to **Venting** to release any remaining pressure. When the floating valve drops, remove the lid and fluff the bulgur with a fork.

4. Stir in the celery, mint, parsley, and lemon juice and serve warm topped with the walnuts and raisins. Store leftovers in an airtight container for 1 week.

MAKE IT GLUTEN-FREE Replace the bulgur with quinoa and cook as directed.

Per Serving: Calories 218, Fat 9g, Carbohydrates 31g, Fiber 5g, Protein 5g

Millet "Cornbread"

Millet is a naturally gluten-free grain containing essential minerals, like magnesium and potassium, that may promote healthy blood pressure levels. I think it tastes remarkably like corn, with slightly more protein per serving. I used ground millet in this recipe to replicate the boxed cornbread mix my mother used to make. It's lightly sweet and goes perfectly with the Two-Bean Chili on page 77.

1. In a mixing bowl, combine the millet flour, baking soda, salt, and coconut sugar and whisk well. Add the pumpkin puree, eggs, and melted coconut oil and whisk until a smooth batter forms.

2. Grease a 7-inch round pan with olive oil and line the pan with parchment paper for easy removal after baking. Pour the batter into the pan and smooth the top with a spatula.

3. Pour 1 cup water into the Instant Pot and arrange the handled trivet (see page 11) on the bottom. Place the pan on top of the trivet and cover it with an upside-down plate or another piece of parchment to protect the bread from condensation. Secure the lid and move the steam release valve to **Sealing**. Select **Manual/Pressure Cook** to cook at high pressure for 30 minutes.

4. When the cooking cycle is complete, quickly release the pressure by moving the steam release valve to **Venting**. When the floating valve drops, remove the lid. Use oven mitts to lift the trivet and the pan out of the pot. Allow the "cornbread" to cool in the pan for 20 minutes before cutting and serving. Remove leftovers from the pan and store in an airtight container in the fridge for 1 week.

MAKE IT VEGAN Omit the eggs and add 2 tablespoons ground flax or chia seeds, ¼ cup water, and 1 teaspoon raw apple cider vinegar to the batter.

NOTE If you can't locate millet flour, make it at home by grinding dry millet grains in a coffee grinder or blender until you have a very fine texture. Alternatively, masa harina (finely ground corn flour) can be used for more of a classic cornbread flavor, while still being gluten-free.

Per Serving: Calories 153, Fat 9g, Carbohydrates 16g, Fiber 1g, Protein 3g

SERVES 8

Prep: 10 minutes
Pressurize: 6 minutes
Cook: 30 minutes
Quick Release
Total: 46 minutes, plus cooling

¾ cup millet flour (see Note)

½ teaspoon baking soda

½ teaspoon fine sea salt

¼ cup coconut sugar

½ cup pumpkin puree

2 eggs, at room temperature

¼ cup melted coconut oil or butter

Beans from Scratch

MAKES 6 CUPS

Prep: 8 hours soaking
Pressurize: 20 minutes
Cook: 3 to 60 minutes
(varies by bean, see chart
on opposite page)
Natural Release:
15 minutes
Total: Varies by bean

**1 pound dried beans
(about 2¼ cups)**

12 cups water

Beans are a staple in my home, both as a side dish and as a hearty addition to the entrée. Whether you soak them or not, they cook much faster in the Instant Pot than they would on the stove top. Soaking beans in water not only speeds their cooking time but it also may help reduce the phytic acid content, which may cause some digestive difficulty. If you forget to soak your beans ahead of time try the quick-soak method (see the opposite page), or if you want to skip the soaking process entirely, cover the dried beans with 2 inches of water and increase the cooking time according to the following chart.

1. Pour the beans in a large bowl (use your unplugged Instant Pot, if you like) and add 6 cups of the water. Let the beans soak on the counter for roughly 8 hours, or place them in the fridge to soak overnight. Drain the soaked beans in a colander and rinse with fresh water.

2. Add the drained beans to the Instant Pot along with the remaining 6 cups water, which should completely cover the beans. Secure the lid and move the steam release valve to **Sealing**. Select **Manual/Pressure Cook** to cook at high pressure according to the chart. (The cooking time varies depending on the type of bean you use.)

3. When the cooking cycle is complete, let the pressure naturally release for 15 minutes, then move the steam release valve to **Venting** to release any remaining pressure. When the floating valve drops, remove the lid.

4. Make sure the beans are tender by mashing one against the side of the pot with a fork. If they are not yet tender, secure the lid and cook for 5 minutes more at high pressure until done. (I naturally release each time so foam doesn't spurt out of the vent and make a mess on my kitchen counter.)

5. Drain the beans in a colander and use them right away, or store them in 1½-cup portions to replace a can of beans in recipes that call for precooked ones. Store cooked beans in an airtight container in the fridge for 1 week, or in the freezer for 3 months.

NOTES Don't overfill the pot. Because beans expand and sometimes foam when cooked, don't fill your Instant Pot more than halfway full when cooking beans from scratch or you might clog the Instant Pot's vent.

Don't cook the beans with salt or acid. Dried beans and other legumes may never become tender if you cook them with salt, soy sauce, vinegar, lemon juice, or other acids. Cook them with water only and add the seasonings later.

Older beans take longer to soften while they cook, so be sure to check the tenderness after the initial cooking time and cook longer if necessary.

QUICK-SOAK METHOD Combine the dried beans and soaking water in the Instant Pot and secure the lid. Move the steam release valve to **Sealing**. Select **Manual/Pressure Cook** to cook at high pressure for 2 minutes. Let the pressure naturally release for 10 minutes, then move the steam release valve to **Venting** to release any remaining pressure. When the floating valve drops, remove the lid. Drain the beans, then use them as you would soaked beans in a recipe.

BEAN / LEGUME	MINUTES AT HIGH PRESSURE, SOAKED	MINUTES AT HIGH PRESSURE, UNSOAKED	RELEASE
Adzuki	4–6	16–20	15 minutes
Black Beans	10–15	22–30	15 minutes
Black-Eyed Peas	5–10	10–15	15 minutes
Cannelini Beans	10–15	30–35	15 minutes
Chickpeas (Garbanzo Beans)	12–15	45–60	15 minutes
Great Northern Beans	7–8	25–30	15 minutes
Kidney Beans	10–15	25–30	15 minutes
Lentils, brown or green	——	4–5	10 minutes
Lentils, red	——	3	5 minutes
Lima Beans	3–6	12–14	15 minutes
Navy Beans	10–15	20–25	15 minutes
Pinto Beans	10–15	25–30	15 minutes
Soybeans	18–20	35–45	15 minutes
Split Peas	——	5–10	10 minutes

CHAPTER

3

Soups
& Stews

Thai Coconut Carrot Soup

This vibrant soup has the perfect balance of sweetness and spice, and is a delicious way to get more nutrients into your diet. Carrots and sweet potatoes are rich in antioxidants, as well as vitamins A, C, and K, and together they make this soup naturally sweet and creamy. I've kept the seasoning mild to appeal to a variety of palates (including my children's), but go ahead and add more ginger or curry powder if you like it spicy.

1. Press **Sauté** and add the olive oil to the Instant Pot. Once the oil is hot but not smoking, add the onion and sauté until tender, about 8 minutes, stirring occasionally so it doesn't stick. Meanwhile, peel and chop the carrots and sweet potatoes into 1-inch chunks.

2. Once the onion is tender, add the garlic, curry powder, and ginger and stir with a wooden spoon or spatula just until fragrant, about 1 minute. Add the carrots, sweet potatoes, water, and salt and use the spoon to scrape the bottom of the Instant Pot to make sure nothing has stuck. Press **Cancel**, then secure the lid and move the steam release valve to **Sealing**. Select **Manual/Pressure Cook** to cook on high pressure for 10 minutes.

3. When the cooking cycle is complete, let the pressure naturally release for 10 minutes before moving the steam release valve to **Venting**. When the floating valve drops, remove the lid and use an immersion blender to blend the soup directly in the pot until very smooth.

4. Stir in the coconut milk and adjust the seasonings to taste. Serve warm with 1 tablespoon each dried cranberries, pumpkin seeds, and cilantro sprinkled over each serving. Store leftovers in an airtight container in the fridge for 5 days.

Per Serving: Calories 221, Fat 9g, Carbohydrates: 32g, Fiber 6g, Protein 11g

SERVES 6

Prep: 5 minutes
Pressurize: 15 minutes
Cook: 19 minutes
Natural Release: 10 minutes
Total: 49 minutes

1 tablespoon extra-virgin olive oil

½ yellow onion, chopped

1 pound carrots

1 pound sweet potatoes

2 cloves garlic, minced

2 teaspoons curry powder

1 tablespoon minced fresh ginger (about 1-inch knob)

3½ cups water

2 teaspoons fine sea salt

½ cup full-fat coconut milk (see page 8)

6 tablespoons dried cranberries

6 tablespoons hulled pumpkin seeds

6 tablespoons chopped fresh cilantro

Broccoli Cheese Soup

SERVES 4

Prep: 7 minutes
Pressurize: 10 minutes
Cook: 3 minutes
Quick Release
Total: 20 minutes

1 yellow onion, chopped

2 carrots, peeled and chopped

1 small head (8 ounces) cauliflower, cut into florets (about 3 cups)

1 pound broccoli, cut into florets (about 6 cups)

1 tablespoon spicy brown mustard

3 cups water

Fine sea salt

½ cup shredded sharp Cheddar cheese

¼ cup finely grated Parmesan cheese

½ cup almond milk, or any milk of your choice

Freshly ground black pepper

This broccoli cheese soup has the comforting flavors you love, without the flour, butter, and heavy cream. Instead, it gets its creaminess from cauliflower and almond milk, which go almost unnoticed once everything is blended together and the cheese is added. When you use an immersion blender, this is a fast one-pot recipe that packs 17 grams of protein per serving.

1. Combine the onion, carrots, cauliflower, broccoli, mustard, water, and 2 teaspoons salt in the Instant Pot. Secure the lid and move the steam release valve to **Sealing**. Select **Manual/Pressure Cook** to cook on high pressure for 3 minutes.

2. When the cooking cycle is complete, immediately move the steam release valve to **Venting** to quickly release the pressure. When the floating valve drops, remove the lid. Use an immersion blender to blend the soup, leaving as much texture as you like.

3. Add the Cheddar, Parmesan, and almond milk and stir until combined. Season with salt and pepper to taste, then serve warm. Store leftovers in an airtight container in the fridge for 5 days.

MAKE IT VEGAN Omit the cheeses and stir in ¼ cup nutritional yeast and 1 tablespoon freshly squeezed lemon juice when you add the almond milk. You may want to add a little more salt, to taste.

Per Serving: Calories 233, Fat 12g, Carbohydrates 13g, Fiber 5g, Protein 17g

Two-Bean Chili

This vegetarian chili makes a filling and affordable meal that's perfect for cold weather. Dried beans cook in a fraction of the time in the Instant Pot, and using two types of beans provides a variety of nutrients and textures. Sweet potatoes add even more nutrients to the mix, and I love how they thicken this soup slightly, making it feel hearty.

1. Drain the soaked beans and rinse well. Combine the beans, onion, carrots, celery, garlic, chili powder, cumin, cayenne, water, tomatoes with their juices, sweet potato, and several grinds of black pepper in the Instant Pot. Stir well to make sure the beans are submerged in the liquid, then secure the lid and move the steam release valve to **Sealing**. Select **Manual/Pressure Cook** to cook on high pressure for 25 minutes.

2. When the cooking cycle is complete, let the pressure naturally release for 10 minutes, then move the steam release valve to **Venting** to release any remaining pressure. When the floating valve drops, remove the lid and add the salt. Stir well, using the back of the spoon to mash some of the sweet potatoes against the side of the pot to thicken the chili.

3. Adjust the seasonings to taste, and serve immediately with green onions and cilantro on top. Store leftovers in an airtight container in the fridge for 1 week.

NOTE If you don't have time to soak your beans, use the quick-soak method described on page 69 and proceed as instructed. To use canned beans, replace the 2 cups dried beans with 6 cups cooked beans (four 15-ounce cans in total). Use only 1 cup water and cook at high pressure for 10 minutes. Let the pressure naturally release for 10 minutes, then remove the lid and serve.

Per Serving: Calories 252, Fat 0g, Carbohydrates 50g, Fiber 28g, Protein 15g

SERVES 6

Prep: 10 minutes, plus soaking
Pressurize: 15 minutes
Cook: 25 minutes
Natural Release: 10 minutes
Total: 1 hour

1 cup dried black beans, soaked for 8 hours (see Note)

1 cup dried red kidney beans, soaked for 8 hours (see Note)

1 yellow onion, chopped

3 carrots, peeled and chopped

3 celery stalks, chopped

4 cloves garlic, minced

1 tablespoon chili powder

2 teaspoons ground cumin

¼ teaspoon cayenne pepper

2 cups water

One 28-ounce can diced tomatoes (see page 10)

1 sweet potato, peeled and cut into 1-inch chunks

Freshly ground black pepper

2 teaspoons fine sea salt

Chopped green onions, tender white and green parts only, for garnish (optional)

Chopped fresh cilantro, for garnish (optional)

Comforting "Noodle" Soup

SERVES 4

Prep: 10 minutes
Pressurize: 15 minutes
Cook: 16 minutes
Quick Release
Total: 37 minutes

1 tablespoon extra-virgin olive oil

1 yellow onion, chopped

3 cloves garlic, minced

1 teaspoon dried thyme, or 2 teaspoons fresh thyme

½ teaspoon dried oregano

1 pound boneless, skinless chicken thighs

3 carrots, peeled and chopped

3 celery stalks, chopped

Fine sea salt and freshly ground black pepper

4 cups (1 quart) low-sodium vegetable broth

1 pound zucchini (about 2 medium)

Chopped fresh flat-leaf parsley, for garnish

Chicken noodle soup is classic comfort food. In this version, it gets a nutritional upgrade by replacing the refined pasta with zucchini "noodles." Because they cook so quickly, stir these vegetable-based noodles into the soup just before serving for a fast low-carb meal.

1. Press **Sauté** and add the olive oil to the Instant Pot. Once the oil is hot but not smoking, add the onion and sauté until softened, about 3 minutes. Add the garlic, thyme, and oregano and cook until fragrant, about 1 minute more, then press **Cancel** to stop the cooking cycle.

2. Add the chicken, carrots, celery, 2 teaspoons salt, several grinds of pepper, and the broth to the pot. Secure the lid and move the steam release valve to **Sealing**. Select **Manual/Pressure Cook** to cook on high pressure for 12 minutes.

3. Meanwhile, use a spiralizer or vegetable peeler to cut noodlelike strips from the zucchini; set the noodles aside.

4. When the cooking cycle is complete, quickly release the pressure by moving the steam release valve to **Venting**. When the floating valve drops, remove the lid. Use tongs to transfer the cooked chicken to a cutting board, then use two forks to shred the chicken.

5. Add the shredded chicken and zucchini noodles to the pot, and stir well. The noodles will soften quickly from the heat. Season with additional salt and pepper, to taste, and serve immediately with parsley on top.

MAKE IT AHEAD You can prepare the soup, minus the zucchini noodles, up to 3 days in advance. When you're ready to serve, warm the soup in a pot over medium-high heat until heated through, about 8 minutes. Add the zucchini noodles just before serving (because they may fall apart with reheating).

MAKE IT VEGAN Replace the chicken with 3 cups cooked chickpeas and 1 tablespoon soy sauce (or tamari, to make it gluten-free) and sauté with the onion. Add the vegetables and seasonings and continue as instructed.

Per Serving: Calories 215, Fat 8g, Carbohydrates 11g, Fiber 4g, Protein 24g

Wild Rice & Mushroom Stew

The flavor of this creamy and comforting stew reminds me of Thanksgiving stuffing, but with more protein and vegetables. Wild rice has twice the amount of protein as brown rice, but is most commonly available as a wild rice and brown rice blend in stores, so that's what I've called for here. If you can find wild rice by itself, the cooking time is the same, so feel free to use that if you prefer. Aside from some chopping of vegetables to get started, all you have to do is add the ingredients to the Instant Pot and press a button.

1. Combine the onion, carrots, celery, garlic, mushrooms, thyme, sage, rice, 4 cups of the water, and 2 teaspoons salt in the Instant Pot and secure the lid. Move the steam release valve to **Sealing** and select **Manual/Pressure Cook** to cook on high pressure for 25 minutes.

2. When the cooking cycle is complete, let the pressure naturally release for 10 minutes, then move the steam release valve to **Venting** to release any remaining pressure. When the floating valve drops, remove the lid. Stir in the coconut milk.

3. Season with additional salt and pepper, to taste, and serve immediately with a squeeze of fresh lemon to brighten the flavors and a few sprigs of thyme. Store leftovers in an airtight container in the fridge for 5 days.

Per Serving: Calories 156, Fat 3g, Carbohydrates 31g, Fiber 4g, Protein 4g

SERVES 6

Prep: 10 minutes
Pressurize: 15 minutes
Cook: 25 minutes
Natural Release: 10 minutes
Total: 1 hour

1 yellow onion, chopped

5 carrots, peeled and chopped

5 celery stalks, chopped

3 cloves garlic, minced

8 ounces cremini mushrooms, roughly chopped

1 teaspoon dried thyme

1 teaspoon ground sage

1 cup wild rice and brown rice blend, or wild rice

4 cups water

Fine sea salt

½ cup full-fat coconut milk (see page 8)

Freshly ground black pepper

Lemon wedges, for serving

Fresh thyme, for garnish

Chipotle Black Bean Soup

SERVES 8

Prep: 10 minutes, plus soaking
Pressurize: 15 minutes
Cook: 20 minutes
Natural Release: 10 minutes
Total: 55 minutes

1 pound dried black beans, soaked for 8 hours (see page 68)

1 yellow onion, chopped

1½ cups chopped carrots (about 3 carrots)

1 cup chopped celery (about 3 stalks)

1 chipotle pepper, canned in adobo sauce, chopped

1 clove garlic, minced

3½ cups water

2 teaspoons ground cumin

2 teaspoons fine sea salt

Chopped fresh cilantro and green onion, for garnish

Lime wedges, for serving

Black beans are an inexpensive form of protein loaded with fiber, vitamins, and minerals, like calcium and iron. This hearty soup, which is seasoned with canned chipotle peppers in adobo sauce for a subtle smoky and spicy flavor, makes enough to feed a crowd.

1. Drain the black beans and combine them with the onion, carrots, celery, chipotle pepper, garlic, water, and cumin in the Instant Pot. Stir well to make sure the beans are submerged in the liquid, then secure the lid and move the steam release valve to **Sealing**. Select **Manual/Pressure Cook** to cook on high pressure for 20 minutes.

2. When the cooking cycle is complete, let the pressure naturally release for 10 minutes. Move the steam release valve to **Venting** to release any remaining pressure. When the floating valve drops, remove the lid. Test the beans to make sure they are tender by pressing one against the side of the pot with a fork. It should be easily mashed. If they are not done, secure the lid again, making sure the sealing ring is properly seated, and cook at high pressure for 10 minutes more. Let the pressure naturally release for 10 minutes so the soup doesn't sputter out of the steam release valve when you move it to **Venting**.

3. Once you're sure the beans are tender, add the salt, then use an immersion blender to blend the soup, leaving as much texture as you like. Alternatively, transfer 2 cups of the soup to a blender and blend until smooth, then return the blended soup to the pot and stir it in. (If your soup is too thick, add a little more water to thin it out.) Taste and adjust the seasonings as needed. For more spice, add some of the canned adobo sauce that was packed with the chipotle peppers, 1 teaspoon at a time, to taste.

4. Serve immediately with cilantro and green onion on top and a squeeze of lime juice. Store leftovers in an airtight container in the fridge for 1 week.

NOTE If you don't have time to soak your beans ahead of time, use the quick-soak method on page 69. To use unsoaked dried beans, add another 2 cups water, cook at high pressure for 60 minutes, then continue as directed. To use cooked black beans, replace the dried beans with 6 cups cooked beans (four 15-ounce cans, drained), use only 2 cups water, then continue as directed.

Per Serving: Calories 167, Fat 0g, Carbohydrates 31g, Fiber 8g, Protein 11g

Lentil Minestrone

Minestrone is typically made with pasta, but in this version, I've used protein-rich lentils instead. As a result, this soup is brimming with fiber and nutrients, and is hearty enough to serve as a main course. Be warned that this recipe makes quite a bit of soup, which is a benefit if you like to meal-prep for the week. If you're only cooking for one or two people and don't want too many leftovers, go ahead and cut this recipe in half.

1. Press **Sauté** and add the olive oil to the Instant Pot. Once the oil is hot but not smoking, add the onion, carrots, and celery and sauté for 5 minutes, until softened. Press **Cancel** and stir in the garlic while the pot is still hot.

2. Add the zucchini, lentils, tomatoes with their juices, basil, oregano, thyme, water, and several grinds of pepper. Give the mixture a stir to ensure the lentils are covered in liquid for even cooking. Secure the lid and move the steam release valve to **Sealing**. Select **Manual/Pressure Cook** and cook on high pressure for 5 minutes.

3. When the cooking cycle is complete, let the pressure naturally release for 10 minutes, then move the steam release valve to **Venting** to release any remaining pressure. When the floating valve drops, remove the lid. Stir in the salt, then taste and adjust the seasonings as needed. Serve immediately, with a squeeze of fresh lemon to brighten the flavors. Store leftovers in an airtight container in the fridge for 5 days.

NOTE If you add salt or another acidic ingredient to the water when cooking lentils, they may never become tender. Don't add salt, tamari, soy sauce, vinegar, or lemon juice to a lentil recipe until *after* the lentils have become tender, which they will do quickly in the Instant Pot.

Per Serving: Calories 238, Fat 4g, Carbohydrates 41g, Fiber 22g, Protein 16g

SERVES 6

Prep: 10 minutes
Pressurize: 15 minutes
Cook: 10 minutes
Natural Release:
10 minutes
Total: 45 minutes

1 tablespoon extra-virgin olive oil

1 yellow onion, chopped

1½ cups chopped carrots (about 3 carrots)

1 cup chopped celery (about 3 stalks)

3 cloves garlic, minced

Heaping 1 cup chopped zucchini (about 1 squash)

1 cup green lentils (see Note)

One 28-ounce can diced tomatoes (see page 10)

2 teaspoons dried basil

1 teaspoon dried oregano

1 teaspoon dried thyme

3 cups water

Freshly ground black pepper

2 teaspoons fine sea salt

Lemon wedges, for serving (optional)

African Peanut Stew

SERVES 8

Prep: 10 minutes
Pressurize: 12 minutes
Cook: 15 minutes
Natural Release:
10 minutes
Total: 47 minutes

1 tablespoon extra-virgin olive oil

1 yellow onion, chopped

2 cloves garlic, minced

2 tablespoons minced fresh ginger (2-inch knob)

1 sweet potato, peeled and cut into 1-inch chunks

One 15-ounce can diced tomatoes (see page 10)

½ cup all-natural peanut butter

2 teaspoons fine sea salt

½ teaspoon red pepper flakes

¼ cup red quinoa, rinsed

3 to 4 cups water

2 cups finely chopped kale, stems removed

Loaded with nutrients, African peanut stew has a unique flavor that my family finds addictive. The combination of ginger and peanut butter reminds me of a slightly spicy Thai peanut sauce, with an earthy sweetness from the sweet potato. I use red quinoa in this stew because it retains its texture better than other varieties, but any color will do for the added plant-based protein.

1. Press **Sauté** and add the olive oil to the Instant Pot. Once the oil is hot but not smoking, add the onion and sauté until softened, about 5 minutes. Press **Cancel** and stir in the garlic and ginger while the pot is still hot.

2. Add the sweet potato, tomatoes with their juices, peanut butter, salt, red pepper flakes, quinoa, and 3 cups of the water, without stirring. (The peanut butter will blend in as the soup cooks.) Secure the lid and move the steam release valve to **Sealing**. Select **Manual/Pressure Cook** to cook on high pressure for 10 minutes.

3. When the cooking cycle is complete, let the pressure naturally release for 10 minutes, then move the steam release valve to **Venting** to release any remaining pressure. When the floating valve drops, remove the lid. Stir in the kale, which should wilt quickly.

4. For a thicker stew, press some of the cooked sweet potatoes against the side of the pot and stir them in until you have a creamier texture. If you like a thinner soup, add up to 1 cup of the remaining water. Taste and adjust the seasoning as needed (I usually add another ½ teaspoon salt), and serve warm. Store leftovers in an airtight container in the fridge for 1 week.

Per Serving: Calories 174, Fat 10g, Carbohydrates 19g, Fiber 3g, Protein 5g

Creamy Tomato Soup

This lightened-up tomato soup gets its creaminess from an unexpected source: butternut squash. Squash becomes ultra-tender when cooked under pressure, so it blends seamlessly into this soup, adding a natural sweetness and velvety texture. Use frozen butternut squash that has already been peeled and cut to make the prep work for this recipe a snap.

1. Press **Sauté** and add the olive oil to the Instant Pot. Once the oil is hot but not smoking, add the onion and sauté until softened, about 5 minutes. Press **Cancel** and stir in the garlic while the pot is still hot.

2. Add the squash, tomatoes with their juices, basil, salt, and water to the pot. Secure the lid and move the steam release valve to **Sealing**. Select **Manual/ Pressure Cook** to cook on high pressure for 5 minutes.

3. When the cooking cycle is complete, let the pressure naturally release for 10 minutes, then move the steam release valve to **Venting**. When the floating valve drops, remove the lid. Stir in the coconut milk. Taste the soup and add the maple syrup, if more sweetness is needed.

4. Use an immersion blender to blend the soup directly in the pot, or carefully transfer the soup to a blender in batches and blend to your desired texture. Taste and adjust the seasoning as needed, then serve warm with basil on top and a few grinds of black pepper. Store leftovers in an airtight container in the fridge for 5 days.

Per Serving: Calories 150, Fat 8g, Carbohydrates 21g, Fiber 3g, Protein 3g

SERVES 4

Prep: 10 minutes
Pressurize: 10 minutes
Cook: 10 minutes
Natural Release:
10 minutes
Total: 40 minutes

1 tablespoon extra-virgin olive oil

1 yellow onion, chopped

1 clove garlic, minced

1 pound frozen peeled and cubed butternut squash

One 28-ounce can diced tomatoes (see page 10)

2 teaspoons dried basil

2 teaspoons fine sea salt

2 cups water

½ cup full-fat coconut milk (see page 8)

1 tablespoon pure maple syrup (see page 10; optional)

Chopped fresh basil, for garnish (optional)

Freshly ground black pepper

Meal-Sized
Salads & Bowls

Thai-Style Farro Salad

With a texture similar to rice, farro is an ancient grain that packs nearly 8 grams of protein and heart-healthy fiber in each cooked cup. (That's even more than quinoa!) Tossed with fresh vegetables and a flavorful dressing, this hearty salad is one of my favorite ways to enjoy farro. I chop the vegetables while the farro is cooking to be as time efficient as possible.

1. Combine the farro and water in the Instant Pot and give it a stir. Secure the lid and move the steam release valve to **Sealing**. Select **Manual/Pressure Cook** to cook on high pressure for 10 minutes. When the cooking cycle is complete, let the pressure naturally release for 10 minutes to fully cook the farro.

2. While the farro is cooking, stir together the olive oil, lime juice, salt, soy sauce, and maple syrup in a small bowl to make a dressing. Seed and chop the red bell pepper, chop the cucumber, peel and shred the carrot, and chop the green onions.

3. After 10 minutes have passed, move the steam release valve to **Venting** to release any remaining pressure. When the floating valve drops, remove the lid. Use oven mitts to lift the stainless-steel insert out of the pot to allow the farro to cool, about 15 minutes.

4. Stir the dressing into the cooked farro, along with the bell pepper, cucumber, carrot, green onions, and cilantro. Transfer the salad to a large airtight container, or into individual containers for easy packed lunches, and chill in the fridge for 2 hours before serving to allow the flavors to fully develop. Store leftovers in the fridge for 5 days.

MAKE IT GLUTEN-FREE Use tamari instead of soy sauce, and replace the farro with 2 cups quinoa. Cook the quinoa at high pressure for 1 minute and let the pressure naturally release for 15 minutes before removing the lid. Alternatively, use any other grain you like for this recipe, using the cooking times found on the chart on page 189.

Per Serving: Calories 354, Fat 7g, Carbohydrates 61g, Fiber 6g, Protein 12g

SERVES 6

Prep: 4 minutes
Pressurize: 10 minutes
Cook: 10 minutes
Natural Release: 10 minutes
Total: 34 minutes, plus chilling

2 cups farro

2 cups water

2 tablespoons extra-virgin olive oil

½ cup freshly squeezed lime juice

1 teaspoon fine sea salt

2 tablespoons soy sauce or tamari

¼ cup pure maple syrup (see page 10)

1 red bell pepper

1 English cucumber

1 large carrot

5 green onions, tender white and green parts only

1 cup loosely packed chopped fresh cilantro

Crunchy Lentil Salad with Shallot Vinaigrette

SERVES 6

Prep: 5 minutes
Pressurize: 10 minutes
Cook: 4 minutes
Natural Release:
10 minutes
Total: 29 minutes,
plus chilling

1½ cups green lentils

2 cups water

¼ cup raw apple cider vinegar

2 tablespoons extra-virgin olive oil

1½ teaspoons fine sea salt

Freshly ground black pepper

1 tablespoon spicy brown mustard

1 tablespoon pure maple syrup (see page 10)

1 clove garlic, minced

¼ cup minced shallots (2 small shallots)

1 English cucumber

1 red bell pepper

½ cup lightly packed chopped fresh flat-leaf parsley

¾ cup raisins

¾ cup sliced almonds

Leafy greens, like arugula, for serving

This refreshing salad is packed with plant-based protein thanks to the green lentils, which cook in just a fraction of the time it would take on the stove. It reminds me of a classic pasta salad tossed with a tangy shallot vinaigrette, but I love that it uses satisfying lentils instead of pasta for a more nutrient-packed alternative. Chop your vegetables as the lentils cook to be as efficient with your time as possible, then enjoy this chilled salad as an easy packed meal all week long.

1. Combine the lentils and water in the Instant Pot and secure the lid, moving the steam release valve to **Sealing**. Select **Manual/Pressure Cook** to cook on high pressure for 4 minutes. When the cooking cycle is complete, let the pressure naturally release for 10 minutes to fully cook the lentils.

2. While the lentils are cooking, stir together the vinegar, olive oil, salt, several grinds of pepper, the mustard, maple syrup, garlic, and shallots in a large bowl to make a dressing. Dice the cucumber (you should have around 2 cups) and add it to the bowl of dressing to marinate. Seed and dice the red bell pepper and add it and the parsley to the bowl of dressing to marinate.

3. After 10 minutes have passed, move the steam release valve to **Venting** to release any remaining pressure. When the floating valve drops, remove the lid.

4. Pour the cooked lentils into a fine-mesh sieve and rinse with cold water to quickly cool them off. Add the cooked lentils to the bowl with the dressing and vegetables and toss well to coat. Stir in the raisins and almonds, then chill in the fridge for 1 hour.

5. Once the salad is chilled, taste and adjust the seasoning as needed. Serve the lentil salad along with the leafy greens. Store leftovers in an airtight container in the fridge for 5 days.

Per Serving: Calories 273, Fat 11g, Carbohydrates 44g, Fiber 13g, Protein 13g

Taco Salad with Zesty Lime Vinaigrette

This salad is hearty enough to serve as a main entrée, thanks to the use of whole-grain barley and black beans, which are both loaded with fiber and plant-based protein. Paired with a zesty lime vinaigrette and your favorite taco toppings, this meal is bursting with bright flavors. Every bite is interesting, which keeps you coming back for more. Chop the vegetables for the salad while the barley is cooking to save time.

1. Combine the barley, water, cumin, chili powder, salsa, and salt in the Instant Pot and stir to combine. Secure the lid and move the steam release valve to **Sealing**. Select **Manual/Pressure Cook** and cook on high pressure for 20 minutes. Let the pressure naturally release for 10 minutes.

2. While the barley is cooking, prepare the vinaigrette. In a pint-sized mason jar, combine the olive oil, vinegar, lime juice, maple syrup, garlic, cumin, cayenne, salt, and several grinds of pepper. Screw on the lid and shake vigorously to combine. Set aside.

3. When the screen reads L0:10, move the steam release valve to **Venting** to release any remaining pressure. When the floating valve drops, remove the lid and stir in the black beans to create the taco "meat." (If using canned beans, drain and rinse them first.)

4. To serve, place the romaine, cabbage, tomatoes, green onions, cilantro, and barley and black bean mixture in a serving bowl. Generously drizzle the lime vinaigrette on top, add a sprinkling of cheese and avocadeo slices, and serve right away. Store leftovers in three separate airtight containers—one each for the "meat," the dressing, and the chopped vegetables—in the fridge for 5 days.

MAKE IT GLUTEN-FREE Replace the barley with 1 cup rinsed quinoa. Cook at high pressure for only 1 minute, then let the pressure naturally release for 15 minutes before venting.

Per Serving: Calories 350, Fat 16g, Carbohydrates 51g, Fiber 10g, Protein 14g

SERVES 6

Prep: 5 minutes
Pressurize: 6 minutes
Cook: 20 minutes
Natural Release: 10 minutes
Total: 41 minutes

1 cup barley

1 cup water

1 teaspoon ground cumin

1 teaspoon chili powder

½ cup prepared salsa

½ teaspoon fine sea salt

1½ cups cooked or canned black beans

2 romaine hearts, chopped

2 cups shredded red cabbage

1 cup cherry tomatoes, halved

½ cup chopped green onions, tender white and green parts only

½ cup chopped fresh cilantro

½ cup crumbled feta or shredded Cheddar cheese

Avocado slices, for garnish

ZESTY LIME VINAIGRETTE

¼ cup extra-virgin olive oil

3 tablespoons raw apple cider vinegar

¼ cup freshly squeezed lime juice

3 tablespoons pure maple syrup (see page 10)

1 clove garlic, minced

1 teaspoon ground cumin

⅛ teaspoon cayenne pepper

½ teaspoon fine sea salt

Freshly ground black pepper

Greek Chickpea Salad

SERVES 6

Prep: 5 minutes, plus soaking
Pressurize: 15 minutes
Cook: 12 minutes
Natural Release: 15 minutes
Total: 47 minutes, plus chilling

1 cup dried chickpeas, soaked for 8 hours (see Note)

3 cups water

¼ cup freshly squeezed lemon juice

2 cloves garlic, minced

2 tablespoons extra-virgin olive oil

½ teaspoon fine sea salt

Freshly ground black pepper

½ red onion, diced

1 English cucumber, diced

1 red bell pepper, seeded and diced

1 cup cherry tomatoes, quartered

½ cup chopped fresh dill

½ cup Kalamata olives, pitted and sliced (optional)

½ cup crumbled feta cheese (optional)

Chickpeas make a satisfying addition to a classic Greek salad as they are loaded with fiber, protein, and complex carbohydrates. If you want to be extra efficient with your time, chop the vegetables as the chickpeas cook. Paired with crunchy cucumbers, sweet bell peppers, and tangy lemon juice, each bite has a different taste and texture to keep things interesting. The addition of fresh dill and creamy feta make this salad totally addictive.

1. Drain the soaked chickpeas and add them to the Instant Pot with the water. Secure the lid and move the steam release valve to **Sealing**. Select **Manual/Pressure Cook** to cook on high pressure for 12 minutes.

2. While the chickpeas are cooking, stir together the lemon juice, garlic, olive oil, salt, and several grinds of black pepper in a large mixing bowl to make a dressing. Add the onion, cucumber, bell pepper, tomatoes, dill, and olives and let them marinate in the dressing until the chickpeas are done.

3. When the cooking cycle is complete, let the pressure naturally release for 15 minutes, then move the steam release valve to **Venting** to release any remaining pressure. When the floating valve drops, remove the lid. Drain and rinse the cooked chickpeas in cold water, then drain again well. Add the chickpeas to the mixing bowl and toss well to coat in the dressing. Add the feta, then taste and adjust the seasonings as needed.

4. Chill the salad in the fridge for 30 minutes before serving to let the flavors meld. Store leftovers in an airtight container in the fridge for 5 days.

NOTE Soaking dried beans is thought to improve digestion and mineral absorption, and speeds the cooking process, but if you forget or don't have time to soak them, use the quick-soak method on page 69. Alternatively, you can cook the dried chickpeas with an additional 1 cup of water on high pressure for 50 minutes, then let the pressure naturally release for 20 minutes before venting and removing the lid. Follow the rest of the recipe as instructed.

Per Serving (with feta and olives): Calories 216, Fat 16g, Carbohydrates 31g, Fiber 12g, Protein 12g

"Cheeseburger" Salad with Special Sauce

Believe it or not, this salad tastes like a cheeseburger without the ground beef or refined white-flour bun. Instead, it's topped with a mixture of lentils and walnuts, which are surprisingly meatlike when seasoned properly (I promise!). Top this off with your favorite burger fixings and the special sauce—and you and your family will be licking the bowl clean. This salad is delicious served warm or cold, so it also makes a great packed lunch.

1. To make the burger "meat," press **Sauté** and add the olive oil to the Instant Pot. Once the oil is hot but not smoking, add the onion and sauté until softened, about 5 minutes. Press **Cancel** to stop the cooking cycle.

2. Stir in the garlic powder, paprika, cayenne, cumin, and black pepper while the pot is still hot. Add the green lentils and water, and stir to make sure the lentils are covered in the liquid for even cooking. Secure the lid and move the steam release valve to **Sealing**. Select **Manual/Pressure Cook** to cook on high pressure for 5 minutes.

3. While the lentils are cooking, make the special sauce. Drain and rinse the cashews, then add them to a blender with the water, vinegar, maple syrup, tomato paste, mustard, onion powder, and salt. Blend until very smooth and set aside.

4. When the cooking cycle on the burger "meat" is complete, let the pressure naturally release for 10 minutes, then move the steam release valve to **Venting** to release any remaining pressure. When the floating valve drops, remove the lid and stir in the salt and chopped walnuts.

5. Fill a bowl with chopped lettuce, the burger "meat," tomatoes, green onions, pickles, and cheese. Drizzle plenty of special sauce over the top before serving. Store leftovers in three separate airtight containers—for the dressing, the burger "meat," and the vegetables—in the fridge for 1 week.

MAKE IT VEGAN Omit the Cheddar cheese.

Per Serving (with 2 tablespoons special sauce): Calories 334, Fat 15g, Carbohydrates 37g, Fiber 17g, Protein 16g

---

SERVES 6

Prep: 15 minutes, plus soaking
Pressurize: 10 minutes
Cook: 10 minutes
Natural Release: 10 minutes
Total: 45 minutes

BURGER "MEAT"

1 tablespoon extra-virgin olive oil

1 yellow onion, chopped

1 teaspoon garlic powder

1 teaspoon paprika

⅛ teaspoon cayenne pepper

½ teaspoon ground cumin

¼ teaspoon freshly ground black pepper

1 cup green lentils

1¼ cups water

1 teaspoon fine sea salt

½ cup finely chopped raw walnuts

SPECIAL SAUCE

½ cup raw cashews, soaked for 1 hour

½ cup water

1 tablespoon raw apple cider vinegar

2 tablespoons pure maple syrup (see page 10)

2 tablespoons tomato paste

2 tablespoons yellow mustard

½ teaspoon onion powder

¾ teaspoon fine sea salt

Chopped lettuce, tomatoes, and green onions; pickle slices; and shredded Cheddar cheese, for serving

Curried Broccoli & White Bean Salad

SERVES 6

Prep: 5 minutes, plus soaking
Pressurize: 12 minutes
Cook: 25 minutes
Natural Release: 10 minutes
Total: 52 minutes, plus cooling

1 cup dried navy beans, soaked for 8 hours (see page 68)

2 cups water

1 head broccoli

1 large carrot

5 green onions, tender white and green parts only

Small handful of fresh cilantro

½ cup dried cranberries (see Note; optional)

½ cup sliced almonds (optional)

CURRIED TAHINI DRESSING

¼ cup tahini

¼ cup freshly squeezed lemon juice

2 tablespoons pure maple syrup (see page 10)

1 clove garlic, minced

2 teaspoons curry powder

1 teaspoon minced fresh ginger (about ½-inch knob)

1 teaspoon fine sea salt

Freshly ground black pepper

This hearty salad gets its creaminess from tahini, a paste made from calcium-rich sesame seeds. Combining crunchy broccoli and protein-rich white beans, this salad will leave you feeling satisfied for hours.

1. Drain the soaked navy beans and add them to the Instant Pot with the water. Secure the lid, and move the steam release valve to **Sealing**. Select **Manual/Pressure Cook** to cook on high pressure for 25 minutes. When the cooking cycle is complete, let the pressure naturally release for 10 minutes, then move the steam release valve to **Venting** to release any remaining pressure.

2. While the beans are cooking, finely chop the broccoli (you should have around 4 cups) and shred the carrot (about 1 cup), adding them to a large mixing bowl as you work. Chop the green onions (about 1 cup) and cilantro (about ½ cup), but leave them on the cutting board for now.

3. To make the dressing, in a separate small bowl, combine the tahini, lemon juice, maple syrup, garlic, curry powder, ginger, salt, and several grinds of black pepper. Whisk well to combine, then add water, 1 tablespoon at a time, and whisk until the dressing is creamy and easy to pour.

4. When the floating valve on the Instant Pot drops, remove the lid. Use a fork to mash a bean against the side of the pot to be sure it is tender. If the beans don't mash easily, secure the lid (be sure the sealing ring is properly seated in the lid) and cook at high pressure for 5 minutes more. Let the pressure naturally release for 10 minutes so no foam spurts from the vent, then test the beans for tenderness again. When ready, drain the beans and add them to the bowl with the broccoli and carrots. Stir well and let the beans cool for 15 minutes; the heat from the beans will soften the broccoli slightly.

5. Once cool, stir in the green onions, cilantro, cranberries, and almonds and pour the dressing over the top. Toss well to coat evenly. Serve right away, or chill the salad in the fridge for 1 hour to let the flavors meld. Store leftovers in an airtight container in the fridge for 3 days.

NOTE Look for dried cranberries that are naturally sweetened with fruit juice, such as Made in Nature and Eden Foods brands.

Per Serving: Calories 234, Fat 10g, Carbohydrates 42g, Fiber 14g, Protein 12g

Wild Rice & Kale Salad

Wild rice has a wonderfully nutty flavor and is rich in antioxidants, which may help to lower the risk of heart attack and slow down the aging process. When paired with kale, which has more iron than beef per calorie, and tossed with lemon juice, red bell peppers, and tomatoes, which are all a great source of vitamin C, this salad is loaded with flavor and nutrients. Since kale is such a sturdy green, you can even dress this salad and use leftovers for packed lunches throughout the week.

1. Add the wild rice and water to the Instant Pot. Secure the lid and move the steam release valve to **Sealing**. Select **Manual/Pressure Cook** and cook on high pressure for 22 minutes.

2. While the rice is cooking, in a large bowl, whisk together the olive oil, lemon juice, garlic, salt, pepper, and maple syrup to make a dressing and set aside.

3. Remove the ribs from the kale and finely chop the leaves (you should have about 2 cups); add the kale to the bowl. Chop the green onions (about 1 cup) and cut the tomatoes into quarters, adding both to the bowl as you work. Seed and chop the red bell pepper and add it to the bowl. Toss the vegetables to coat well in the dressing.

4. When the cooking cycle is complete, let the pressure naturally release for 10 minutes, then move the steam release valve to **Venting** to release any remaining pressure. When the floating valve drops, remove the lid. Give the rice a stir and add it to the bowl of dressed vegetables. (If you haven't finished chopping the vegetables, you can finish as the rice cools.) Toss well to coat, then chill the bowl in the fridge for 30 minutes.

5. Just before serving, stir in the feta and taste and adjust the seasonings as needed, adding an extra squeeze of lemon juice to brighten the flavors. Store leftovers in an airtight container in the fridge for 3 days.

Per Serving: Calories 206, Fat 12g, Carbohydrates 21g, Fiber 4g, Protein 7g

SERVES 4

Prep: 5 minutes
Pressurize: 6 minutes
Cook: 22 minutes
Natural Release: 10 minutes
Total: 43 minutes, plus chilling

1 cup wild rice, or wild and brown rice blend (see headnote, page 81)

1¼ cups water

2 tablespoons extra-virgin olive oil

¼ cup freshly squeezed lemon juice, plus more as needed

1 clove garlic, minced

½ teaspoon fine sea salt

¼ teaspoon freshly ground black pepper

2 teaspoons pure maple syrup (see page 10)

1 small bunch kale

5 green onions, tender white and green parts only

1 cup cherry tomatoes

1 red bell pepper

½ cup crumbled feta cheese

Korean Chicken Bowls

SERVES 4

Prep: 10 minutes
Pressurize: 6 minutes
Cook: 12 minutes
Natural Release:
10 minutes
Total: 38 minutes

⅓ cup soy sauce
(or tamari, to make it
gluten-free)

5 tablespoons pure maple
syrup (see page 10)

1 teaspoon minced fresh
ginger (about ½-inch
knob)

1 tablespoon Sriracha

1 clove garlic, minced

1 pound boneless, skinless
chicken breasts

1 cup white rice, such
as jasmine or basmati,
rinsed

1 cup water, plus
2 tablespoons

1 red bell pepper

½ red onion

1 cup fresh baby spinach

1 tablespoon arrowroot
starch (see page 8)

½ cup chopped green
onions, tender white
and green parts only
(about 3 onions)

Sesame seeds, for garnish

This flavorful Korean-inspired sauce is hard to resist. To be as efficient as possible, I cook the rice along with the chicken. This is called "pot-in-pot" cooking (see page 16). If you prefer a lower-carb option, skip the rice and serve the cooked chicken and vegetables over Easy Cauliflower "Rice" (page 56).

1. Add the soy sauce, maple syrup, ginger, Sriracha, and garlic to the Instant Pot and stir to combine. Place the chicken on top of the sauce in a single layer. To cook the rice at the same time, position a 2.5-inch trivet (see page 12) over the chicken breasts and place a 7-inch oven-safe bowl on top. Add the rice and 1 cup water to the bowl, then secure the lid and move the steam release valve to **Sealing**. Select **Manual/Pressure Cook** to cook on high pressure for 4 minutes.

2. While the chicken and rice are cooking, seed the red pepper and slice it thinly. Slice the onion thinly into half-moons, and chop the spinach.

3. When the cooking cycle is complete, let the pressure naturally release for 10 minutes, then move the steam release valve to **Venting** to release any remaining pressure. When the floating valve drops, remove the lid. Use oven mitts to lift the trivet and the bowl of cooked rice out of the pot. Use tongs to transfer the chicken to a cutting board to rest. Press **Cancel** to stop the cooking cycle.

4. Add the sliced bell pepper and onion to the sauce in the Instant Pot. Press **Sauté** and let the vegetables simmer in the sauce until crisp-tender, about 5 minutes. In a small bowl, whisk together the arrowroot with the remaining 2 tablespoons water to create a slurry. While the vegetables are cooking, use two forks to shred the chicken, then add it back to the pot once the vegetables are tender. Stir in the baby spinach until it wilts, about 1 minute. Stir in the arrowroot slurry and continue stirring until the sauce thickens, 1 to 2 minutes.

5. Serve the chicken and vegetables over the cooked rice with a sprinkling of green onions and sesame seeds over the top. Store leftovers in an airtight container in the fridge for 3 or 4 days.

MAKE IT VEGAN Omit the chicken and arrowroot slurry. Cook 1 cup green lentils with 1¼ cups water on high pressure for 5 minutes along with the rice. Add the sauce and vegetables to the cooked lentils, and simmer as directed.

Per Serving: Calories 268, Fat 4g, Carbohydrates 31g, Fiber 2g, Protein 24g

Cold Sesame Noodle Bowls

This cold noodle bowl is a great way to ease into eating more vegetables. To make this a complete meal, I include shrimp, which you can quickly sauté in your Instant Pot after the pasta is finished cooking. You can add any other protein you like, such as salmon, chicken, tofu, or cooked chickpeas.

1. Place the spaghetti in the Instant Pot, crisscrossing the noodles as you add them to prevent large clumps of pasta from sticking together. Pour the water over the noodles, making sure they are covered for even cooking. Secure the lid and move the steam release valve to **Sealing**. Select **Manual/Pressure Cook** to cook on high pressure for 2 minutes.

2. While the noodles are cooking, in a large bowl, stir together the lime juice, 2 tablespoons of the soy sauce, the maple syrup, sesame oil, ginger, and garlic. Add the cabbage, carrot, and green onions and toss well to coat.

3. When the cooking cycle is complete, let the pressure naturally release for 10 minutes, then move the steam release valve to **Venting** to release any remaining pressure. Press **Cancel** to stop the cooking cycle. When the floating valve drops, remove the lid and drain the pasta through a colander. Rinse the pasta with cold water to stop the cooking process.

4. Dry the pot with a towel, then return the pot to the Instant Pot housing to cook the shrimp. Press **Sauté** and add the olive oil to the Instant Pot. Once the oil is hot but not smoking, add the shrimp and the remaining 1 tablespoon soy sauce and sauté until pink and tender, about 4 minutes. (If using frozen shrimp, you'll need to cook it for 2 to 3 minutes more.)

5. Add the noodles and cooked shrimp to the bowl and toss well to coat. Taste and adjust the seasoning as needed; add a squeeze of Sriracha if you like spice. Serve with sesame seeds sprinkled over the top. Store leftovers in an airtight container in the fridge for 4 days.

MAKE IT GLUTEN-FREE Use tamari instead of soy sauce, and replace the whole-wheat spaghetti with a gluten-free variety, like brown rice or a legume-based spaghetti. Cook gluten-free pasta at high pressure for 0 minutes (see page 17), and let the pressure naturally release for 8 minutes.

Per Serving: Calories 327, Fat 8g, Carbohydrates 43g, Fiber 4g, Protein 23g

SERVES 4

Prep: 14 minutes
Pressurize: 10 minutes
Cook: 6 minutes
Natural Release: 10 minutes
Total: 40 minutes

4 ounces whole-wheat spaghetti, broken in half

4 cups water

2 tablespoons freshly squeezed lime juice

3 tablespoons soy sauce or tamari

2 tablespoons pure maple syrup (see page 10)

1 tablespoon sesame oil

1 tablespoon minced fresh ginger (about 1-inch knob)

1 clove garlic, minced

½ head red cabbage, shredded (about 1 pound)

1 cup shredded carrot (about 1 large carrot)

½ cup chopped green onions, tender white and green parts only (about 3 onions)

1 tablespoon extra-virgin olive oil

1 pound fresh or frozen raw shrimp, peeled and deveined

Sriracha (optional)

Sesame seeds, for garnish

Roasted Vegetable Bowls

SERVES 6

Prep: 18 minutes
Pressurize: 6 minutes
Cook: 26 minutes
Natural Release:
15 minutes
Total: 1 hour
5 minutes

1 pound sweet potatoes,
cut into 1-inch chunks

Extra-virgin olive oil,
for drizzling

Fine sea salt and freshly
ground black pepper

1 pound brussels sprouts,
cleaned and halved

1 bunch asparagus, cut
into 1-inch pieces with
woody stems removed
(optional)

1 cup quinoa, rinsed

1¼ cups water

6 tablespoons tahini

¼ cup freshly squeezed
lemon juice

2 cloves garlic, minced

1 teaspoon ground cumin

2 cups chopped kale

1 cup cherry tomatoes,
halved

1 cucumber, chopped

When I first started using my Instant Pot, I used it most often for making recipes like this one. The pressure cooker takes care of cooking the quinoa, while vegetables roast to perfection in the oven, leaving your hands free to mix together the dressing.

1. Preheat the oven to 400°F. Arrange the sweet potatoes on a large baking sheet and drizzle with olive oil. Toss the potatoes to coat with the oil, then season with salt and pepper and place them in the oven to roast for 25 minutes.

2. Once the sweet potatoes are in the oven, arrange the brussels sprouts and asparagus on a second large baking sheet and drizzle with olive oil. Toss the sprouts and asparagus to coat with the oil, then season with salt and pepper and place them in the oven along with the sweet potatoes. Roast until the vegetables are tender and golden, 15 to 20 minutes. (Because the sweet potatoes have a head start, everything should finish cooking at roughly the same time.)

3. While the vegetables are roasting, add the quinoa and 1 cup of the water to the Instant Pot and give it a stir. Secure the lid and move the steam release valve to **Sealing**. Select **Manual/Pressure Cook** and cook on high pressure for 1 minute. When the cooking cycle is complete, let the pressure naturally release for 15 minutes.

4. While the quinoa is cooking, in a small bowl, combine the tahini, lemon juice, garlic, cumin, remaining ¼ cup water, ¼ teaspoon salt, and several grinds of pepper. Whisk well (adding more water, 1 tablespoon at a time, as needed to thin).

5. When the screen reads L0:15, move the steam release valve to **Venting** to release any remaining pressure. When the floating valve drops, remove the lid and use a fork to fluff the quinoa.

6. To serve, fill each bowl with some chopped kale, cooked quinoa, roasted vegetables, cherry tomatoes, and cucumber. Drizzle the creamy tahini dressing over the top. Store leftovers in four separate airtight containers—for the quinoa, the roasted vegetables, the raw vegetables, and the dressing—in the fridge for 5 days.

Per Serving (with 2 tablespoons dressing): Calories 439, Fat 18g, Carbohydrates 58g, Fiber 10g, Protein 16g

Eggroll in a Bowl

If you love the flavor of eggrolls but don't want to indulge in the deep-fried wrapper too often, this dish is for you. It puts classic eggroll fillings, like cabbage, carrots, and ground turkey, front and center for a low-carb take on a favorite takeout appetizer. For a quick weeknight dinner, to be as efficient with my time as possible, I quickly chop the vegetables while the turkey is browning.

1. Press **Sauté** and add the olive oil, onion, turkey, and salt to the Instant Pot. Sauté until the turkey is browned and cooked through, breaking it up with a wooden spoon as you stir, about 8 minutes. Press **Cancel** to stop the cooking cycle.

2. Add the soy sauce, carrots, and celery and stir. Add the cabbage on top without stirring. (The cabbage may nearly fill the pot, but it will reduce significantly in size while cooking.) Secure the lid and move the steam release valve to **Sealing**. Select **Manual/Pressure Cook** to cook on high pressure for 0 minutes (see page 17). When the cooking cycle is complete, immediately move the steam release valve to **Venting** to quickly release the steam pressure (so you don't overcook the vegetables).

3. When the floating valve drops, remove the lid and stir together the vegetables and meat to make sure everything is coated in the soy sauce. Stir in the sesame oil and a few grinds of pepper to taste. Taste and adjust the seasonings as needed.

4. Use tongs to transfer the eggroll filling to bowls. Garnish with the sesame seeds and green onions and serve warm. Store leftovers in an airtight container in the fridge for 4 days.

MAKE IT VEGAN Swap 1 pound sliced cremini mushrooms for the ground turkey, sautéing for only 5 minutes in step 1.

MAKE IT GLUTEN-FREE Use tamari instead of soy sauce.

Per Serving: Calories 272, Fat 12g, Carbohydrates 9g, Fiber 4g, Protein 25g

---

SERVES 4

Prep: 10 minutes
Pressurize: 8 minutes
Cook: 8 minutes
Quick Release
Total: 26 minutes

1 tablespoon extra-virgin olive oil

1 red onion, chopped

1 pound ground turkey

½ teaspoon fine sea salt

⅓ cup soy sauce or tamari

3 carrots, peeled and shredded

3 celery stalks, chopped

1 small head cabbage, shredded (about 1½ pounds)

1 teaspoon toasted sesame oil

Freshly ground black pepper

Sesame seeds and chopped green onions, tender white and green parts only, for garnish

Vegetarian Comfort Food

Walnut Pesto Pasta

This easy pasta is bursting with flavor, thanks to a quick homemade pesto sauce. Cooking whole-wheat pasta with green lentils provides extra plant-based protein, and I love how you don't need to use much cheese to achieve a classic pesto taste. Stir in any vegetables you have on hand to complete this comforting meal.

1. Pour 4 cups of the water into the Instant Pot, add the pasta and lentils, and stir well to make sure they are submerged in the water for even cooking. Secure the lid and move the steam release valve to **Sealing**. Select **Manual/Pressure Cook** to cook at high pressure for 4 minutes. Let the pressure naturally release for 10 minutes, then move the steam release valve to **Venting** to release any remaining pressure.

2. While the pasta is cooking, combine the arugula, basil, lemon juice, garlic, walnuts, the remaining ¼ cup water, and the salt in the bowl of a food processor or blender and process until a relatively smooth pesto forms.

3. When the floating valve drops, remove the lid and press **Cancel** to stop the cooking cycle. Use oven mitts to remove the pot and drain the cooked pasta and lentils in a fine-mesh sieve. Rinse with cold water to remove some starch and stop the cooking process. Dry the pot with a towel and return it to the Instant Pot housing.

4. Press **Sauté** and add the olive oil to the pot. Once the oil is hot but not smoking, add the tomatoes, zucchini, and artichoke hearts and stir until softened, about 5 minutes. Stir in the drained pasta and lentils and pesto sauce and toss well to coat. Stir in the Parmesan and several grinds of pepper. Taste and adjust the seasonings as needed, then serve warm. Store leftovers in an airtight container in the fridge for 5 days.

MAKE IT VEGAN Omit the cheese, and add 2 to 3 tablespoons nutritional yeast to add a "cheesy" flavor.

MAKE IT GLUTEN-FREE Omit the whole-wheat pasta and use a gluten-free variety, like brown rice or legume-based pasta, and replace the green lentils with red lentils (which cook faster than green lentils). Cook at high pressure for 0 minutes (see page 17) and let the pressure naturally release for 8 minutes.

Per Serving: Calories 385, Fat 15g, Carbohydrates 48g, Fiber 12g, Protein 19g

SERVES 6

Prep: 10 minutes
Pressurize: 6 minutes
Cook: 9 minutes
Natural Release: 10 minutes
Total: 35 minutes

4¼ cups water

8 ounces whole-wheat pasta, like rotini or penne

½ cup green lentils

1 cup lightly packed arugula

1 cup lightly packed fresh basil leaves

2 tablespoons freshly squeezed lemon juice

2 or 3 cloves garlic, minced

½ cup raw walnut halves

1 teaspoon fine sea salt

1 tablespoon extra-virgin olive oil

1½ cups cherry tomatoes, halved

1 zucchini, chopped

One 15-ounce can artichoke hearts, drained and rinsed

¼ cup grated Parmesan cheese

Freshly ground black pepper

Hidden Cauliflower Mac 'n' Cheese

SERVES 8

Prep: 7 minutes
Pressurize: 15 minutes
Cook: 3 minutes
Natural Release:
10 minutes
Total: 35 minutes

1 pound whole-wheat
macaroni

4 cups water

2 tablespoons soy sauce
or tamari

1 tablespoon spicy brown
mustard

1½ teaspoons fine sea salt

1 pound fresh or frozen
cauliflower florets

4 ounces extra-sharp
Cheddar cheese

¼ cup grated Parmesan
cheese, or other cheese of
your choice, like Gruyère

I love to sneak vegetables into my favorite comfort foods, and this mac 'n' cheese fits the bill. The cauliflower becomes so tender that it completely dissolves into the sauce when stirred—no additional equipment needed. I've seasoned this so you can use less cheese than traditional recipes, but be sure to use an extra-sharp Cheddar to maximize the cheesy flavor.

1. Pour the pasta into the Instant Pot and add the water, soy sauce, mustard, and salt. Stir well to combine, then add the cauliflower on top without stirring, making sure that the cauliflower layer completely covers the pasta for even cooking. Secure the lid and move the steam release valve to **Sealing**. Select **Manual/Pressure Cook** to cook on high pressure for 3 minutes. While the pot is coming to pressure, shred the Cheddar (you should have about 1 cup).

2. When the cooking cycle is complete, let the pressure naturally release for 10 minutes, then move the steam release valve to **Venting** to release any remaining pressure.

3. When the floating valve drops, remove the lid and stir the pasta well, using a spatula to break up any pasta that has stuck together or stuck to the bottom of the pot. (A little sticking is to be expected, but it will loosen up when you stir.) Use the spatula to mash any intact cauliflower florets against the side of the pot to help them dissolve into the pasta sauce.

4. Add the Cheddar and Parmesan and stir well. Adjust the seasonings as needed and serve warm. Store leftovers in an airtight container in the fridge for 4 days.

MAKE IT VEGAN Use store-bought vegan cheese, or make a cashew "cheese" sauce. Soak 1 cup raw cashews for 1 hour, then drain and rinse. In a blender, combine 2 cups of the water with the cashews, 2 tablespoons freshly squeezed lemon juice, and ¼ cup nutritional yeast. Blend on high speed until smooth. Add the blended mixture to the Instant Pot, along with the remaining 2 cups water and the rest of the ingredients. Cook as directed. Stir in an additional ½ cup water after cooking for a creamier sauce.

MAKE IT GLUTEN-FREE Omit the macaroni and soy sauce, and use gluten-free pasta and tamari instead. Use only 3 cups water and cook on high pressure for 0 minutes (see page 17). Let the pressure naturally release for 8 minutes, then continue as directed above.

Per Serving: Calories 305, Fat 10g, Carbohydrates 43g, Fiber 7g, Protein 18g

Instant "Fried Rice"

Traditional fried rice is tossed in lots of oil and uses minimal vegetables. I've turned the dish on its head with this healthier version, making vegetables the star of the show. When seasoned with soy sauce, garlic, and ginger, some of my family members can't even tell that the rice is made of cauliflower!

1. Press **Sauté** and add the olive oil to the Instant Pot. Once the oil is hot but not smoking, add the onion, carrots, and celery and sauté until softened, about 4 minutes. Stir in the garlic and ginger and sauté just until fragrant, about 1 minute more. Press **Cancel** to stop the cooking cycle.

2. Add the cauliflower, soy sauce, and salt. Secure the lid and move the steam release valve to **Sealing**. Select **Manual/Pressure Cook** to cook on high pressure for 0 minutes (see page 17).

3. When the cooking cycle is complete, immediately move the steam release valve to **Venting** to quickly release the steam pressure. This prevents the cauliflower from overcooking. When the floating valve drops, remove the lid and use a potato masher or fork to break up the cauliflower into small ricelike pieces. (It's okay if you end up breaking up some of the other veggies, too.)

4. Press **Cancel** to stop the cooking cycle, then press **Sauté**. Add the peas and give the rice a stir to combine. The peas will cook quickly.

5. Use a spatula to move the mixture to the edges of the pan, creating a clear space in the center of the pot to scramble the eggs. Since there will be some liquid covering the bottom of the pot, crack the eggs into the liquid so you don't have to use additional oil for cooking. Using a spatula, scramble the eggs as they cook until fluffy and cooked through, about 3 minutes. (This should also help evaporate some of that liquid.)

6. Mix the scrambled eggs into the "fried rice" mixture and stir in the sesame oil. Taste and adjust the seasonings as needed. Serve warm with the green onions and sesame seeds sprinkled over the top. Store leftovers in an airtight container in the fridge for 4 days.

MAKE IT GLUTEN-FREE Use tamari instead of soy sauce.

Per Serving: Calories 253, Fat 10g, Carbohydrates 27g, Fiber 7g, Protein 15g

SERVES 4

Prep: 12 minutes
Pressurize: 8 minutes
Cook: 8 minutes
Quick Release
Total: 28 minutes

1 tablespoon extra-virgin olive oil, plus more as needed

1 red onion, chopped

3 carrots, peeled and chopped

3 celery stalks, chopped

1 clove garlic, minced

1 teaspoon minced fresh ginger (about ½-inch knob)

2 pounds cauliflower, cut into small florets

⅓ cup soy sauce or tamari

½ teaspoon fine sea salt

1 cup fresh or frozen peas

4 eggs

1 teaspoon sesame oil

Chopped green onions, tender white and green parts only, for garnish

Sesame seeds, for garnish

Mushroom & Barley "Risotto"

SERVES 4

Prep: 10 minutes
Pressurize: 10 minutes
Cook: 25 minutes
Natural Release:
10 minutes
Total: 55 minutes

1 tablespoon extra-virgin
olive oil

1 yellow onion, chopped

8 ounces cremini
mushrooms, chopped

2 cloves garlic, minced

1 teaspoon dried thyme

1 cup pearled barley

½ cup dried black-eyed
peas, unsoaked

2 cups water

1 teaspoon fine sea salt

1 tablespoon soy sauce
or tamari

1 generous handful baby
spinach

1 tablespoon freshly
squeezed lemon juice

¼ cup grated Parmesan
cheese, plus more for
serving

Traditional risotto can be a labor-intensive process as you stand over the stove stirring, but the Instant Pot makes risotto pretty darn hands-off. Instead of using white rice, this recipe calls for pearled barley, which contains more fiber and nutrients, and has a creamy texture similar to risotto. Adding dried black-eyed peas, which cook along with the barley, makes this a complete and filling meal. If you're not a fan of mushrooms, use another sturdy vegetable, like sweet potatoes or butternut squash, in their place, plus any other seasonings you like, such as fresh sage or rosemary. These options will become very tender and may partially dissolve into the sauce, making the resulting "risotto" even more creamy.

1. Press **Sauté** and add the olive oil to the Instant Pot. Once the oil is hot but not smoking, add the onion and mushrooms and sauté until the onion is softened, about 5 minutes. Press **Cancel** and stir in the garlic while the pot is still hot.

2. Add the thyme, barley, peas, and water and stir well. Secure the lid and move the steam release valve to **Sealing**. Select **Manual/Pressure Cook** and cook on high pressure for 20 minutes.

3. When the cooking cycle is complete, let the pressure naturally release for 10 minutes, then move the steam release valve to **Venting** to release any remaining pressure. When the floating valve drops, remove the lid.

4. Stir in the salt, soy sauce, spinach, lemon juice, and Parmesan until the spinach wilts and the cheese melts. Taste and adjust the seasoning as needed, and serve immediately with additional Parmesan on the side. Store leftovers in an airtight container in the fridge for 5 days.

MAKE IT VEGAN Omit the Parmesan and season with additional salt and lemon juice, to taste. Add ¼ cup nutritional yeast for an extra "cheesy" flavor, if you like.

MAKE IT GLUTEN-FREE Use tamari instead of soy sauce and replace the barley with brown rice. Increase the pressure cooking time to 22 minutes, then blend the rice with an immersion blender after cooking to create a creamy texture, if desired.

Per Serving: Calories 322, Fat 6g, Carbohydrates 55g, Fiber 11g, Protein 15g

Kung Pao Chickpeas

In this dish inspired by Chinese takeout, chickpeas are cooked in a flavorful sauce that will rival your favorite restaurant. I developed this recipe to use ingredients I always have in my pantry, including canned chickpeas, to make it an easy one to throw together on a busy weeknight. Be sure to use a syrupy balsamic vinegar for the best flavor. And for a meal that's lower in carbs, replace the rice with Easy Cauliflower "Rice" (page 56).

1. Combine the onion, bell pepper, chickpeas, soy sauce, vinegar, maple syrup, ginger, garlic, ¾ teaspoon of the red pepper flakes, and ⅓ cup of the water in the Instant Pot and stir well.

2. Arrange a 2.5-inch trivet (see page 12) over the chickpeas and place a 7-inch oven-safe bowl on top. Add the rice and 1 cup of the water to the bowl. Secure the lid and move the steam release valve to **Sealing**. Select **Manual/Pressure Cook** to cook on high pressure for 4 minutes.

3. When the cooking cycle is complete, let the pressure naturally release for 10 minutes, then move the steam release valve to **Venting** to release any remaining pressure. Remove the lid and use oven mitts to lift the trivet and the bowl out of the pot. Fluff the rice with a fork.

4. In a separate small bowl, stir together the arrowroot with the remaining 2 tablespoons water to make a slurry. Stir the slurry into the hot chickpeas. The sauce should thicken and become glossy within 1 to 2 minutes.

5. Stir in the sesame oil and green onions. Serve the chickpeas and sauce over the rice garnished with the sesame seeds. Store leftovers in an airtight container in the fridge for 5 days.

MAKE IT GLUTEN-FREE Use tamari instead of soy sauce.

Per Serving (with rice): Calories 350, Fat 4g, Carbohydrates 67g, Fiber 11g, Protein 15g

SERVES 4

Prep: 10 minutes
Pressurize: 10 minutes
Cook: 6 minutes
Natural Release: 10 minutes
Total: 36 minutes

½ red onion, chopped

1 red bell pepper, seeded and chopped

3 cups cooked chickpeas, or two 15-ounce cans chickpeas, drained and rinsed

6 tablespoons soy sauce or tamari

2 tablespoons aged balsamic vinegar

3 tablespoons pure maple syrup (see page 10)

1 tablespoon minced fresh ginger (about 1-inch knob)

1 clove garlic, minced

¾ to 1 teaspoon crushed red pepper flakes

1⅓ cups plus 2 tablespoons water

1 cup long-grain white rice, like jasmine or basmati, rinsed

1 tablespoon arrowroot starch (see page 8)

1 teaspoon toasted sesame oil

1 cup chopped green onions, tender white and green parts only

Sesame seeds, for garnish

Eggplant Parmesan Casserole

SERVES 6

Prep: 15 minutes
Pressurize: 10 minutes
Cook: 9 minute
Natural Release:
15 minutes
Total: 49 minutes

1 tablespoon extra-virgin olive oil

1 yellow onion, chopped

8 ounces cremini mushrooms, chopped

2 cloves garlic, minced

1 eggplant, cut into 1-inch cubes

½ teaspoon fine sea salt

½ cup water

1 cup quinoa, rinsed

One 25-ounce jar marinara sauce

¼ cup grated Parmesan cheese

½ cup shredded fresh mozzarella cheese

Chopped fresh parsley, for garnish

Eggplant can be an intimidating vegetable to prep and cook, but it doesn't get much easier than this casserole. Instead of deep-frying the eggplant, or coating individual slices in bread crumbs and cheese, cubes of eggplant cook to tender perfection in the Instant Pot, along with protein-rich quinoa and mushrooms. This has similar flavors to the classic Italian dish with just a fraction of the cheese and no refined flour for better health.

1. Press **Sauté** and add the olive oil to the Instant Pot. Once the oil is hot but not smoking, add the onion and mushrooms and sauté until the onion is softened, about 5 minutes. Press **Cancel**, then add the garlic, eggplant, and salt while the pot is still hot. Stir briefly with a wooden spoon to distribute the salt.

2. Add the water and quinoa, then use the spoon to scrape the bottom of the pot to make sure nothing has stuck. Pour the marinara sauce over the top without stirring. Secure the lid and move the steam release valve to **Sealing**. Select **Manual/Pressure Cook** to cook on high pressure for 1 minute.

3. When the cooking cycle is complete, let the pressure naturally release for 15 minutes, then move the steam release valve to **Venting** to release any remaining pressure. When the floating valve drops, remove the lid and stir in the Parmesan. Turn on your oven's broiler.

4. Transfer the mixture to a 9 by 13-inch casserole dish or a 12-inch oven-safe skillet and smooth the top with a spatula. Sprinkle the mozzarella over the top, place the dish under the broiler, and broil until the cheese is bubbly and lightly golden, 2 to 3 minutes.

5. Garnish with the parsley and serve warm. Store leftovers in an airtight container in the fridge for 1 week.

MAKE IT VEGAN Omit the cheese, or use your favorite vegan cheese, instead.

Per Serving: Calories 309, Fat 10g, Carbohydrates 44g, Fiber 7g, Protein 14g

Spicy Lentil Burgers

Most veggie burger recipes require you to own a food processor or to roast veggies for nearly an hour before you even get started. With the Instant Pot, you don't need that kind of time or any additional equipment to make these spicy lentil-based burgers. The lentils cook in less than 10 minutes in the Instant Pot and then you simply bake the patties all at once, giving you a quick meal made for a crowd (or a very hungry family). Serve with your favorite bun and burger toppings, or wrap these patties in lettuce leaves, or use them to top a salad for an even healthier version.

1. Combine the lentils and water in the Instant Pot and stir to make sure the lentils are submerged in the water. Sprinkle the mushrooms over the top without stirring. Secure the lid and move the steam release valve to **Sealing**. Select **Manual/Pressure Cook** to cook on high pressure for 3 minutes.

2. When the cooking cycle is complete, let the pressure naturally release for 5 minutes, then move the steam release valve to **Venting** to release any remaining pressure. When the floating valve drops, remove the lid. Give the lentils and mushrooms a stir (the lentils should have a mushy texture), then use oven mitts to remove the metal insert from the Instant Pot and let the mixture cool for 10 minutes.

3. Preheat the oven to 375°F and line a large baking sheet with parchment paper. Stir in the cumin, diced red onion, cilantro, Sriracha, salt, and oats into the mashed lentil mixture. Using a ⅓-cup measuring cup, scoop the batter onto the lined baking sheet. Wet your hands, then shape the batter into ½-inch-thick patties, spaced evenly on the baking sheet.

4. Bake the patties for 20 minutes. Use a spatula to carefully flip the patties and bake for 10 minutes more, or until the edges feel firm. Remove the baking sheet from the oven and let the patties cool on the pan for 10 minutes to help them firm up even more.

5. To serve, place each patty on a bun and top with lettuce, tomatoes, sliced red onion, ketchup, and mustard. Store leftover patties in an airtight container in the fridge for 5 days, or in the freezer for 3 months. To reheat, arrange the patties on a baking sheet and warm in a 350°F oven for 10 minutes, until the centers are heated through.

MAKES 8 PATTIES

Prep: 15 minutes
Pressurize: 7 minutes
Cook: 33 minutes
Natural Release:
5 minutes
Total: 1 hour, plus cooling

¾ cup red lentils

1½ cups water

1½ cups finely chopped cremini mushrooms (4 ounces)

1½ teaspoons ground cumin

¼ red onion, finely diced

½ cup lightly packed chopped fresh cilantro

2 tablespoons Sriracha

¾ teaspoon fine sea salt

1 cup quick-cooking oats

Hamburger buns or lettuce leaves, for serving (optional)

Lettuce leaves, sliced tomatoes, sliced red onion, ketchup, and mustard, for topping (optional)

Per Patty: Calories 103, Fat 1g, Carbohydrates 18g, Fiber 3g, Protein 6g

Pad Thai Stir-Fry

SERVES 4

Prep: 5 minutes
Pressurize: 10 minutes
Cook: 7 minutes
Natural Release:
10 minutes
Total: 32 minutes

4 ounces whole-wheat
spaghetti

4 cups water

¼ cup all-natural peanut
butter or almond butter

5 tablespoons soy sauce
or tamari

¼ cup pure maple syrup
(see page 10)

2 tablespoons freshly
squeezed lime juice

1 tablespoon Sriracha

1 teaspoon minced fresh
ginger (about ½-inch
knob)

1 clove garlic, minced

½ head green or red
cabbage, shredded
(about 4 cups)

1 large carrot, shredded

1 red bell pepper, seeded
and chopped

2 cups snow peas

3 green onions, tender
white and green parts
only, chopped

Chopped fresh cilantro,
for garnish

Chopped peanuts or
almonds, for garnish

Pad thai is a popular street dish in Thailand that features noodles tossed in a spicy sauce with crushed peanuts. I rarely have the exotic ingredients required to make an authentic version of this dish at home, so I developed this recipe, which uses ingredients you probably already have in your pantry. To save time, prep your vegetables while the pasta is cooking.

1. Break the spaghetti noodles in half and arrange them in the Instant Pot in a crisscross manner to help avoid clumping. Pour the water over the noodles. Secure the lid and move the steam release valve to **Sealing**. Select **Manual/Pressure Cook** to cook on high pressure for 2 minutes. While the noodles are cooking, in a bowl, whisk together the peanut butter, soy sauce, maple syrup, lime juice, Sriracha, ginger, and garlic and set aside.

2. When the cooking cycle is complete, let the pressure naturally release for 10 minutes, then move the steam release valve to **Venting** to release any remaining pressure.

3. When the floating valve drops, press **Cancel** and remove the lid. Drain the noodles through a colander, rinsing them with cold water to remove some starch and stop the cooking process. Rinse and dry the metal insert and return it to the Instant Pot.

4. Press **Sauté** and pour the peanut sauce into the pot. Add the cabbage, carrot, bell pepper, and snow peas and stir well. Sauté until the vegetables are tender, about 5 minutes. Stir in the drained noodles and the green onions just until everything is heated through. (If the noodles stick together, rinse them again under cold water to unstick them before adding.)

5. Serve the pad thai warm, with the cilantro and peanuts sprinkled over the top. This dish is best served right away, but you can store leftovers in an airtight container in the fridge for 5 days. Use the Instant Pot's sauté function to reheat, or serve the leftovers cold.

MAKE IT GLUTEN-FREE Use tamari instead of soy sauce and replace the whole-wheat pasta with a gluten-free alternative, like brown rice spaghetti. Cook on high pressure for 0 minutes (see page 17), then let the pressure naturally release for 8 minutes before draining.

Per Serving: Calories 242, Fat 9g, Carbohydrates 37g, Fiber 7g, Protein 8g

Lazy Falafel Wraps

Traditional falafel is deep-fried and takes quite a while to prepare. This easier falafel-flavored filling is my healthier solution. Made with quick-cooking lentils and quinoa, this filling can be wrapped in lettuce leaves or stuffed in a pita along with a drizzle of tahini dressing and your favorite Mediterranean toppings for a fast and flavorful meal.

1. Combine the onion, lentils, quinoa, water, garlic, cumin, coriander, and cayenne in the Instant Pot. Secure the lid and move the steam release valve to **Sealing**. Select **Manual/Pressure Cook** to cook on high pressure for 5 minutes.

2. While the lentils are cooking, make the dressing. In a bowl, combine the tahini, lemon juice, 3 tablespoons of the water, the garlic, salt, and several grinds of black pepper. Add up to 1 tablespoon of the remaining water as needed to thin the dressing. Taste and adjust the seasonings as needed.

3. When the cooking cycle is complete, let the pressure naturally release for 10 minutes, then move the steam release valve to **Venting** to release any remaining pressure.

4. When the floating valve drops, remove the lid and stir in the salt, parsley, cilantro, and lemon juice. Taste and adjust the seasonings as needed, adding more lemon juice to brighten the flavors.

5. Spoon the filling into lettuce leaves and top with the sliced cucumber, bell pepper, and carrots. Drizzle the tahini dressing on top and serve. Place leftovers in two separate airtight containers—one each for the filling and the dressing—and store in the fridge for 5 days. Serve warm or chilled.

Per Serving (with 1 tablespoon dressing): Calories 209, Fat 8g, Carbohydrates 27g, Fiber 6g, Protein 9g

SERVES 6

Prep: 10 minutes
Pressurize: 10 minutes
Cook: 5 minutes
Natural Release: 10 minutes
Total: 35 minutes

1 yellow onion, chopped

1 cup green lentils

½ cup quinoa, rinsed

1¾ cups water

2 cloves garlic, minced

2 teaspoons ground cumin

½ teaspoon ground coriander

¼ teaspoon cayenne pepper (optional)

1 teaspoon fine sea salt

½ cup chopped fresh flat-leaf parsley

½ cup chopped fresh cilantro

1 tablespoon freshly squeezed lemon juice, plus more as needed

TAHINI DRESSING

¼ cup tahini

3 tablespoons freshly squeezed lemon juice

3 to 4 tablespoons water

2 cloves garlic, minced

¼ teaspoon fine sea salt

Freshly ground black pepper

Romaine or butter lettuce leaves, for serving

Sliced cucumber, red bell pepper, and carrots, for serving

Speedy Sweet Potato Curry

SERVES 4

Prep: 10 minutes
Pressurize: 10 minutes
Cook: 4 minutes
Natural Release:
3 minutes
Total: 27 minutes

1 tablespoon extra-virgin
olive oil

1 yellow onion, chopped

1 tablespoon curry powder

1 teaspoon ground ginger

3 cups water

2 sweet potatoes, cut into
1-inch chunks

2 carrots, peeled and
chopped

1 cup red lentils (see Note)

1½ teaspoons fine sea salt

Freshly ground black
pepper

½ cup full-fat coconut
milk (see page 8)

1 cup chopped kale, stems
removed

1 tablespoon pure maple
syrup (see page 10;
optional)

Cooked rice, quinoa, or
Easy Cauliflower "Rice"
(page 56), for serving

Chopped fresh cilantro,
for garnish

This simple curry makes a fast weeknight dinner and is a great way to use up any veggies you might have on hand. Because it cooks so quickly, there isn't enough time to cook rice or quinoa in the same pot, but you could easily cook any grain you'd like on the stove before starting the curry, or make Easy Cauliflower "Rice" ahead of time for a grain-free alternative.

1. Press **Sauté** and add the olive oil to the Instant Pot. Once the oil is hot but not smoking, add the onion, curry powder, and ginger and stir just until fragrant, about 1 minute. Press **Cancel** to stop the cooking cycle.

2. Add the water and use a wooden spoon or spatula to scrape the bottom of the pot, making sure nothing has stuck. Add the sweet potatoes, carrots, lentils, salt, and a few grinds of pepper. Stir well to ensure the lentils are covered in water, then secure the lid and move the steam release valve to **Sealing**. Select **Manual/Pressure Cook** to cook on high pressure for 1 minute.

3. When the cooking cycle is complete, let the pressure naturally release for 3 minutes, then move the steam release valve to **Venting**. When the floating valve drops, remove the lid and add the coconut milk and kale. Stir until the kale has wilted, about 2 minutes. Taste and adjust the seasonings as needed, adding the maple syrup if you want a little sweetness.

4. Serve the curry warm over the grain of your choice and garnished with the cilantro. Store leftovers in an airtight container in the fridge for 1 week.

NOTE Red lentils cook much faster than other varieties, so I don't recommend swapping them for green or brown lentils here. You would have to increase the cooking time, which would overcook the other vegetables.

Per Serving (curry only): Calories 259, Fat 8g, Carbohydrates 37g, Fiber 7g, Protein 10g

Lentil & Walnut Tacos

Lentils are low in calories and high in nutrients, and I love how any spices you cook them with get soaked right up. In this case, the lentils taste remarkably similar to real taco meat, but I think the overall texture is even better when you add coarsely ground walnuts for crunch. Together, lentils and nuts provide a great source of plant-based protein and omega-3 fatty acids for a healthier taco night.

1. Combine the lentils, water, cumin, and chili powder in the Instant Pot. Stir well to ensure the lentils are covered in liquid, then sprinkle the onion and canned tomatoes (along with their juices) over the top, without stirring. Secure the lid and move the steam release valve to **Sealing**. Select **Manual/Pressure Cook** to cook on high pressure for 5 minutes.

2. While the lentils are cooking, finely chop the walnuts and chop the lettuce, fresh tomatoes, green onions, and avocado.

3. When the cooking cycle is complete, let the pressure naturally release for 10 minutes, then move the steam release valve to **Venting** to release any remaining pressure. When the floating valve drops, remove the lid and use a fork to mash a lentil against the side of the pot to make sure it's tender. If the lentils aren't tender, secure the lid (be sure the sealing ring is properly seated in the lid) and cook at high pressure for 2 minutes more. Let the pressure naturally release for 5 minutes before venting and removing the lid.

4. Stir in the salt and chopped walnuts. Taste and adjust the seasonings as needed. To serve, spoon the taco "meat" into taco shells, and top with lettuce, tomato, green onion, and avocado. Store leftover taco "meat" in an airtight container in the fridge for 5 days.

MAKE IT GLUTEN-FREE This recipe is naturally gluten-free when served with corn tortillas, or use lettuce wraps as a low-carb and grain-free alternative.

Per Taco (with a corn taco shell): Calories 144, Fat 8g, Carbohydrates 15g, Fiber 4g, Protein 4g

SERVES 6

Prep: 10 minutes
Pressurize: 8 minutes
Cook: 5 minutes
Natural Release: 10 minutes
Total: 33 minutes

1 cup green or brown lentils

1¼ cups water

1 teaspoon ground cumin

1 teaspoon chili powder

1 yellow onion, chopped

One 14-ounce can fire-roasted tomatoes with green chiles

¾ cup walnut halves

Lettuce, tomatoes, green onions, and avocado, or your favorite taco toppings, for serving

1 teaspoon fine sea salt

12 taco shells, for serving

Vegetarian Red Beans & Rice

SERVES 4

Prep: 15 minutes, plus soaking
Pressurize: 10 minutes
Cook: 30 minutes
Natural Release: 10 minutes
Total: 1 hour, 5 minutes

1 cup dried red kidney beans, soaked for 8 hours (see page 68)

2½ cups water

1 yellow onion, chopped

4 celery ribs, chopped

1 red bell pepper, seeded and chopped

4 cloves garlic, minced

1 teaspoon dried thyme

1 teaspoon dried oregano

⅛ teaspoon cayenne pepper

¼ teaspoon freshly ground black pepper

2 tablespoons tomato paste

1 cup long-grain brown rice, rinsed

1 tablespoon soy sauce or tamari

¾ teaspoon fine sea salt

Chopped green onions, tender white and green parts only, for garnish

Chopped fresh cilantro, for garnish

Red beans and rice is a New Orleans dish that makes a hearty and affordable meal, with a spicy kick. Although this still takes a little over an hour plus soaking time, the Instant Pot really simplifies the effort since the rice and beans cook together in the same pot—from scratch! Traditionally, this dish would be made with sausage, bacon, or ham, so go ahead and add some if you miss the meat. I find this vegetarian version to be an equally satisfying plant-based alternative.

1. Pour the drained beans into the Instant Pot, add 1½ cups of the water, and stir to make sure the beans are submerged for even cooking. Without stirring, add the onion, celery, red bell pepper, garlic, thyme, oregano, cayenne, black pepper, and tomato paste on top.

2. Arrange a 2.5-inch trivet (see page 12) over the bean mixture and place a 7-inch oven-safe bowl or pan on top. Add the rice and remaining 1 cup water to the bowl. Secure the lid and move the steam release valve to **Sealing**. Select **Manual/Pressure Cook** to cook on high pressure for 30 minutes.

3. When the cooking cycle is complete, let the pressure naturally release for 10 minutes, then move the steam release valve to **Venting** to release any remaining pressure. When the floating valve drops, remove the lid. Use oven mitts to lift the trivet and the bowl out of the pot. Use a spoon to press a bean against the side of the pot to make sure it's tender. If they need a little more cooking time (which could be the case for older beans), secure the lid (be sure the sealing ring is properly seated) and cook on high pressure for 5 minutes more. Let the pressure naturally release for 10 minutes before venting and removing the lid. When the beans are tender, stir in the soy sauce and salt.

4. For an authentic New Orleans–style dish, use a potato masher to mash some of the beans until the broth thickens to your liking. (If the beans are too liquidy, press **Sauté** and let some of the liquid evaporate.) Taste and adjust the seasonings as needed, then serve the beans with a scoop of brown rice topped with the green onions and cilantro. Store leftovers in an airtight container in the fridge for 1 week.

MAKE IT GLUTEN-FREE Use tamari instead of soy sauce.

Per Serving: Calories 349, Fat 2g, Carbohydrates 69g, Fiber 16g, Protein 17g

One-Pot Shepherd's Pie

Shepherd's pie often requires two pots cooking on the stove at once, but the Instant Pot makes this dish super streamlined. This vegetarian version is loaded with comforting vegetables and protein-packed lentils, which are then topped with fluffy mashed cauliflower for a lighter meal. Because red lentils cook so quickly, they dissolve and naturally thicken the gravy for the filling—without the need for flour or butter.

1. Combine the onion, garlic, carrots, celery, mushrooms, red lentils, water, chickpeas, thyme, rosemary, soy sauce, 1 teaspoon salt, and several grinds of pepper in the Instant Pot and give it a stir.

2. Arrange a 2.5-inch trivet (see page 12) over the vegetables and place a 7-inch oven-safe bowl on top. Add the cauliflower to the bowl. Secure the lid and move the steam release valve to **Sealing**. Select **Manual/Pressure Cook** to cook on high pressure for 5 minutes.

3. When the cooking cycle is complete, let the pressure naturally release for 10 minutes, then move the steam release valve to **Venting** to release any remaining pressure. When the floating valve drops, remove the lid and use oven mitts to lift the trivet and the bowl out of the pot.

4. Stir the filling at the bottom of the pot. Taste and adjust the seasonings as needed. The lentils should dissolve into the sauce as you stir, thickening it. Pour the cooked cauliflower into a large bowl and use a fork or potato masher to mash it until smooth. Generously season the mash with salt and pepper.

5. To serve, spoon the warm filling into bowls and top each with mashed cauliflower. Garnish with fresh herb sprigs and a final grind of pepper. Store leftovers in two separate airtight containers—for the filling and the cauliflower mash—in the fridge for 5 days.

MAKE IT GLUTEN-FREE Use tamari instead of soy sauce.

Per Serving: Calories 221, Fat 2g, Carbohydrates 40g, Fiber 10g, Protein 14g

SERVES 4

Prep: 15 minutes
Pressurize: 6 minutes
Cook: 5 minutes
Natural Release: 10 minutes
Total: 36 minutes

1 yellow onion, chopped

2 cloves garlic, minced

3 carrots, peeled and chopped

3 celery stalks, chopped

8 ounces cremini mushrooms, roughly chopped

½ cup red lentils

1 cup water

1½ cups cooked chickpeas (see pages 68–69), or one 15-ounce can chickpeas, drained and rinsed

1 teaspoon dried thyme, or 2 teaspoons fresh thyme leaves

1 tablespoon minced fresh rosemary

1 tablespoon soy sauce or tamari

Fine sea salt and freshly ground black pepper

1 pound cauliflower, cut into small florets

Fresh rosemary or thyme sprigs, for garnish

CHAPTER

6

Protein-Packed
Favorites

One-Pot Turkey Bolognese with "Spaghetti"

SERVES 4

Prep: 5 minutes
Pressurize: 10 minutes
Cook: 23 minutes
Natural Release:
10 minutes
Total: 48 minutes

1 tablespoon extra-virgin olive oil

1 yellow onion, chopped

2 cloves garlic, minced

1 pound ground turkey

Fine sea salt

One 28-ounce can diced tomatoes (see page 10)

2 celery stalks, diced

2 carrots, diced

1 tablespoon aged balsamic vinegar

1 teaspoon pure maple syrup (see page 10)

½ teaspoon dried oregano

1 teaspoon dried basil

One 3-pound spaghetti squash

¼ cup full-fat coconut milk (see page 8; optional)

Freshly ground black pepper

Fresh basil, for garnish (optional)

This is total comfort food, but with less saturated fat and more veggies than traditional recipes. Using spaghetti squash as the noodles makes this dish lower in carbohydrates and higher in nutrients, and because you cook it all at once along with the sauce, it makes for a convenient weeknight meal.

1. Press **Sauté** and add the olive oil, onion, garlic, turkey, and 1 teaspoon salt to the Instant Pot. Sauté until the turkey is browned and cooked through, breaking it up with a wooden spoon as you stir, about 8 minutes. While the meat is cooking, pour the diced tomatoes with their juices into a blender and blend until smooth. Set aside until the meat is browned.

2. Press **Cancel** to stop the cooking cycle. Add the blended tomatoes, the celery, carrots, vinegar, maple syrup, oregano, basil, and ½ teaspoon salt and stir well.

3. Wash the spaghetti squash and carefully pierce the skin once with a sharp knife to vent. Place the whole squash directly into the sauce, pierced side up. Secure the lid and move the steam release valve to **Sealing**. Select **Manual/Pressure Cook** to cook on high pressure for 15 minutes.

4. When the cooking cycle is complete, let the pressure naturally release for 10 minutes, then move the steam release valve to **Venting** to release any remaining pressure. When the floating valve drops, remove the lid. Use oven mitts to lift the spaghetti squash out of the pot. Transfer it to a cutting board to cool slightly. Stir the coconut milk into the sauce and season with salt and pepper, to taste.

5. Cut the cooked squash in half crosswise and use a spoon to remove the seeds from the center. Use a fork to scrape out "noodles" from the squash and place them on plates. Spoon the Bolognese sauce on top of the noodles and serve. Store leftovers in an airtight container in the fridge for 3 or 4 days.

MAKE IT VEGAN Replace the turkey with lentils. Omit the salt and vinegar so the lentils cook properly. Add 1 cup green lentils and 1 cup water to the vegetables in step 2, then cook as directed. Let the pressure naturally release for 10 minutes before venting. Remove the lid and the cooked squash, then stir in only 1 teaspoon salt, along with the aged balsamic vinegar and coconut milk. Taste and adjust the seasonings as needed, then serve warm.

Per Serving: Calories 271, Fat 12g, Carbohydrates 18g, Fiber 5g, Protein 24g

Thai Salmon Curry

Salmon is loaded with healthy omega-3 fatty acids and cooks very quickly in the Instant Pot, making this Thai-style curry a fast weeknight dinner. While you don't have enough time to cook pot-in-pot rice, you could easily cook any grain on the stove before starting the curry, or make cauliflower "rice" ahead of time for a low-carb meal.

1. Press **Sauté** and add the olive oil to the Instant Pot. Once the oil is hot but not smoking, add the red onion and sauté for 3 minutes, until softened. Add the ginger and curry powder and stir with a wooden spoon for 1 minute more. Press **Cancel** to stop the cooking process.

2. Add a splash of water to the pan, scraping the bottom with the wooden spoon or a spatula to make sure nothing is stuck. Add the bell pepper, coconut milk, maple syrup, lime juice, and soy sauce.

3. Arrange a 2.5-inch trivet (see page 12) on top of the curry and place the salmon on top of the trivet in a single layer, skin side down. Sprinkle the salt and a few grinds of pepper over the fish. Secure the lid and move the steam release valve to **Sealing**. Select **Manual/Pressure Cook** to cook on high pressure for 2 minutes.

4. When the cooking cycle is complete, immediately move the steam release valve to **Venting** to quickly release the steam pressure (so the salmon doesn't overcook). When the floating valve drops, remove the lid. Use a fork to flake the cooked fish directly into the sauce below. The skin will most likely stick to the trivet, making it easy to flake the part you want to eat. Remove any small bones you see, too. Use oven mitts to lift the trivet out of the pot.

5. Press **Cancel**, then press **Sauté** and simmer until the sauce reduces slightly, about 3 minutes. Stir in the basil and riced cauliflower and press **Cancel** to stop the cooking cycle. Serve the curry warm with cilantro sprinkled over the top. Store leftovers in an airtight container in the fridge for 3 days.

MAKE IT VEGAN Omit the salmon and use two 15-ounce cans of cooked chickpeas instead. Add the beans in step 2 and cook as directed.

Per Serving: Calories 432, Fat 30g, Carbohydrates 15g, Fiber 4g, Protein 25g

SERVES 4

Prep: 10 minutes
Pressurize: 5 minutes
Cook: 9 minutes
Quick Release
Total: 24 minutes

1 tablespoon extra-virgin olive oil

½ red onion, chopped

1 tablespoon minced fresh ginger (about 1-inch knob)

1 tablespoon curry powder

1 red bell pepper, seeded and chopped

One 15-ounce can full-fat coconut milk (see page 8)

2 tablespoons pure maple syrup (see page 10)

1 tablespoon freshly squeezed lime juice

1 tablespoon soy sauce (or tamari, to make it gluten-free)

1 pound wild-caught Alaskan salmon

½ teaspoon fine sea salt

Freshly ground black pepper

¼ cup chopped fresh basil

4 cups Easy Cauliflower "Rice" (page 56)

Chopped fresh cilantro or basil, for garnish

Creamy Tuscan Chicken with Mashed "Potatoes"

SERVES 4

Prep: 10 minutes
Pressurize: 5 minutes
Cook: 16 minutes
Quick Release
Total: 31 minutes

1 cup full-fat canned coconut milk (see page 8)

1 pound fresh or frozen cauliflower florets

1 pound boneless, skinless chicken breasts

Fine sea salt and freshly ground black pepper

¼ cup chopped sun-dried tomatoes

½ teaspoon dried basil

½ teaspoon dried oregano

3 cloves garlic, minced

Heaping 1 cup baby spinach or chopped kale

This creamy chicken dish is Italian comfort food at its finest. When you cook cauliflower at the same time as the chicken, the cauliflower becomes extremely tender and easily mashed into a low-carb mash similar to mashed potatoes. Served with a dairy-free garlic cream sauce, this one-pot dinner is totally irresistible.

1. Pour the coconut milk into the Instant Pot and add the cauliflower florets. Place the chicken breasts directly on top of the cauliflower, then sprinkle with ½ teaspoon salt and a few grinds of pepper. Secure the lid and move the steam release valve to **Sealing**. Select **Manual/Pressure Cook** to cook on high pressure for 10 minutes.

2. When the cooking cycle is complete, quickly release the pressure by moving the steam release valve to **Venting**. When the floating valve drops, remove the lid. Use tongs to transfer the chicken to a cutting board to rest. Use oven mitts to lift out the pot and drain the cauliflower, reserving the liquid for the sauce. Pour the drained cauliflower into a separate bowl and set aside.

3. Return the pot to the Instant Pot housing and add the reserved liquid. Press **Cancel**, then press **Sauté**. Add the sun-dried tomatoes, basil, oregano, and garlic and simmer, stirring constantly, for about 5 minutes, until the sauce reduces by about one-third. Taste and add more salt as needed, then stir in the spinach until it wilts, about 1 minute more. Remove the insert from the pot and set it aside so the sauce can cool and thicken a bit more (though it is still a relatively thin sauce that packs a lot of flavor).

4. Use a fork to mash the cauliflower, then season it with salt and pepper to taste. To serve, slice the chicken and place several slices on a plate with some mash. Top them both with a spoonful of the cream sauce, tomatoes, and spinach. Store leftovers in an airtight container in the fridge for 3 or 4 days.

MAKE IT VEGAN Cook the cauliflower as directed above, but omit the chicken. Once cooked, drain the cauliflower, return the reserved cooking liquid to the pot and add 3 cups cooked chickpeas (two 15-ounce cans, drained and rinsed) along with the other sauce ingredients, and continue as directed in step 3, above.

Per Serving: Calories 253, Fat 13g, Carbohydrates 10g, Fiber 5g, Protein 26g

Easy Taco Casserole

If you'd like to change up your usual taco routine, try this quick casserole for a nutrient-rich alternative. When shopping for ground beef, look for an organic brand (from cows raised without the use of antibiotics or hormones) that is 85 to 90 percent lean. Grass-fed beef is naturally lower in fat than its conventional counterpart, and contains more vitamins, antioxidants, and omega-3 fatty acids, but you can also use ground turkey in this dish with similar results.

1. Press **Sauté** and add the olive oil, beef, onion, and salt to the Instant Pot. Sauté until the meat is browned and cooked through, breaking it up with a wooden spoon as you stir, about 8 minutes. Add the garlic, chili powder, and cumin and stir until fragrant, about 1 minute. Press **Cancel** to stop the cooking cycle.

2. Add the water and salsa and stir well, making sure that nothing is stuck on the bottom of the pot. Without stirring, sprinkle the bulgur over the top, making sure it doesn't touch the bottom of the pot (which might give you a "Burn" error). Scatter the bell pepper and black beans over the bulgur to help it cook evenly, then secure the lid and move the steam release valve to **Sealing**. Select **Manual/Pressure Cook** to cook on high pressure for 1 minute.

3. When the cooking cycle is complete, let the pressure naturally release for 10 minutes, then move the steam release valve to **Venting** to release any remaining pressure. When the floating valve drops, remove the lid. Stir the mixture well, then taste and adjust the seasonings as needed.

4. To serve, transfer the mixture to a serving platter and top as desired. Serve warm. Store leftovers in an airtight container in the fridge for 3 or 4 days.

MAKE IT VEGAN Omit the beef and salt in step 1, and add 1 pound sweet potatoes cut into 1-inch chunks and ½ teaspoon salt in step 2. Cook on high pressure for 3 minutes, then continue as directed above. Serve without cheese.

NOTE If you get a "Burn" error while making this, the final dish may still turn out well if the floating valve has already popped up, signaling that the pot has come to pressure. Let the pressure remain in the pot for 10 minutes, to finish cooking the bulgur. Then release the pressure and stir to make sure everything has cooked through.

SERVES 4

Prep: 10 minutes
Pressurize: 8 minutes
Cook: 10 minutes
Natural Release: 10 minutes
Total: 38 minutes

1 tablespoon extra-virgin olive oil

1 pound lean ground beef or turkey

1 red onion, chopped

1 teaspoon fine sea salt

1 clove garlic, minced

1 teaspoon chili powder

1½ teaspoons ground cumin

1 cup water

1½ cups prepared salsa

¾ cup bulgur (or quinoa, to make it gluten-free)

1 green bell pepper, seeded and chopped

1½ cups cooked black beans, or one 15-ounce can black beans, rinsed and drained

Avocado slices, chopped fresh cilantro, chopped lettuce, chopped tomatoes, chopped green onions, and shredded Cheddar cheese, for topping (optional)

Per Serving (without toppings): Calories 346, Fat 6g, Carbohydrates 48g, Fiber 13g, Protein 29g

Mongolian Beef Stir-Fry

SERVES 4

Prep: 5 minutes
Pressurize: 8 minutes
Cook: 11 minutes
Natural Release:
10 minutes
Total: 34 minutes

1 pound skirt steak

⅓ cup soy sauce (or tamari, to make it gluten-free)

3 tablespoons pure maple syrup (see page 10)

1 tablespoon raw apple cider vinegar

1 tablespoon minced fresh ginger (1-inch knob)

2 cloves garlic, minced

5 ounces sliced shiitake mushrooms

1 cup bulgur (or white rice, to make it gluten-free)

1¼ cups plus
2 tablespoons water

2 heads baby bok choy

1 cup sugar snap peas

1 cup shredded carrots

1 tablespoon arrowroot starch (see page 8)

½ cup chopped green onions, tender white and green parts only

Chopped fresh cilantro, for garnish

Sesame seeds, for garnish

I give Mongolian beef a healthy makeover by simmering steak and veggies in a naturally sweetened garlic-ginger sauce. I cook a bowl of whole-grain bulgur at the same time as the beef for an easy one-pot meal. Using 100 percent grass-fed beef naturally lowers the fat content, and I pair this with sliced mushrooms for an extra dose of B vitamins.

1. Use a sharp knife to thinly cut the steak across the grain into ½-inch-thick slices. Place the steak in the Instant Pot and add the soy sauce, maple syrup, vinegar, ginger, garlic, and mushrooms. Stir to coat the beef.

2. In a 7-inch oven-safe bowl, combine the bulgur and 1¼ cups of the water. Arrange a 2.5-inch trivet (see page 12) over the meat and place the bowl on top. Secure the lid and move the steam release valve to **Sealing**. Select **Manual/Pressure Cook** to cook on high pressure for 4 minutes.

3. While the meat and bulgur are cooking, prepare the bok choy. Trim the ends, rinse well to remove any dirt, then slice crosswise into 1-inch pieces.

4. When the cooking cycle is complete, let the pressure naturally release for 10 minutes, then move the steam release valve to **Venting** to release any remaining pressure. When the floating valve drops, remove the lid and press **Cancel** to stop the cooking cycle. Use oven mitts to lift the trivet and the bowl out of the pot. Press **Sauté** and add the bok choy, snap peas, and carrots. Cook, stirring often, until the vegetables are crisp-tender, about 5 minutes.

5. In a separate bowl, stir together the arrowroot and the 2 tablespoons water to make a slurry. Pour the slurry into the pot and stir until the sauce thickens, 1 to 2 minutes. Serve the beef and vegetables over the cooked bulgur with a generous topping of green onions, cilantro, and sesame seeds. Store leftovers in an airtight container in the fridge for 3 or 4 days.

MAKE IT VEGAN Replace the steak with two large sliced portobello mushrooms and cook as directed above.

NOTE For fewer calories and carbohydrates, replace the bulgur and its cooking water with fresh cauliflower florets (use a 7-inch round pan for even cooking). Use a potato masher to mash the cauliflower into "rice" for serving.

Per Serving: Calories 408, Fat 13g, Carbohydrates 33g, Fiber 8g, Protein 38g

Soy-Ginger Salmon with Broccoli

Salmon is an excellent source of protein and omega-3 fatty acids, and it comes to perfection in just minutes in the Instant Pot. Because the broccoli cooks even faster than the fish, you add it at the very end of the cooking process to ensure it doesn't turn to mush. Whip up this addictive soy-ginger dressing while the pot is coming to pressure for an easy 20-minute meal. Serve any extra dressing over a simple salad on the side.

1. Pour 1 cup water into the Instant Pot and arrange the handled trivet (see page 11) on the bottom. Place the salmon fillets on the trivet in a single layer, skin side down. Sprinkle them generously with salt and pepper.

2. Secure the lid and move the steam release valve to **Sealing**. Select **Manual/ Pressure Cook** to cook on high pressure for 0 minutes (see page 17). When the cooking cycle is complete, immediately move the steam release valve to **Venting** to quickly release the steam pressure.

3. While the fish is cooking, make the dressing. Combine the olive oil, soy sauce, vinegar, ginger, garlic, maple syrup, and sesame oil in a blender and blend until smooth, about 1 minute. Set aside until ready to serve.

4. When the floating valve drops, remove the lid and place the broccoli directly on top of the cooked fish. Secure the lid again and move the steam release valve to **Sealing**. Select **Manual/Pressure Cook** to cook on high pressure for 0 minutes. When the cooking cycle is complete, immediately move the steam release valve to **Venting** to quickly release the steam pressure.

5. When the floating valve drops, remove the lid. Use tongs to transfer the steamed broccoli and salmon to serving plates. Drizzle the dressing over the top and garnish with the sesame seeds and green onions. Store leftovers in an airtight container in the fridge for 4 days.

MAKE IT VEGAN Instead of salmon, serve the soy-ginger dressing over a bowl of steamed vegetables and brown rice to make a sushi-style bowl. Roasted red bell peppers have a similar texture to raw fish, so they make an excellent vegan substitute.

MAKE IT GLUTEN-FREE Use tamari instead of soy sauce.

Per Serving (with 2 tablespoons of dressing): Calories 395, Fat 26g, Carbohydrates 14g, Fiber 3g, Protein 27g

SERVES 4

Prep: 5 minutes
Pressurize: 12 minutes
Cook: 1 minute
Quick Release
Total: 18 minutes

1 pound wild-caught Alaskan salmon, cut into four 4-ounce fillets

Fine sea salt and freshly ground black pepper

SOY-GINGER DRESSING

6 tablespoons extra-virgin olive oil

2 tablespoons soy sauce or tamari

2 tablespoons raw apple cider vinegar

1 tablespoon minced fresh ginger (about 1-inch knob)

1 clove garlic

3 tablespoons pure maple syrup (see page 10)

1 teaspoon toasted sesame oil

1 pound broccoli, cut into florets

Sesame seeds, for garnish

Chopped green onions, tender white and green parts only, for garnish

Orange Chicken & Vegetables

SERVES 4

Prep: 10 minutes
Pressurize: 10 minutes
Cook: 22 minutes
Quick Release
Total: 42 minutes

Juice and zest from
1 orange (⅓ cup juice and
about ½ tablespoon zest)

⅓ cup pure maple syrup
(see page 10)

⅓ cup soy sauce or tamari

3 tablespoons raw apple
cider vinegar

1 tablespoon minced fresh
ginger (about 1-inch knob),
or ½ teaspoon dried ginger

1 clove garlic, minced, or
¼ teaspoon ground garlic

¼ teaspoon red pepper
flakes

1 pound boneless, skinless
chicken thighs

1 cup white jasmine rice,
rinsed

1 cup plus 2 tablespoons
water

½ red onion, thinly sliced

1 red bell pepper, seeded
and sliced

2 cups chopped broccoli
florets (about 8 ounces)

1 tablespoon arrowroot
starch (see page 8)

Chopped green onion and
sesame seeds, for garnish
(optional)

Orange chicken is a takeout favorite, but it's far from healthy when the chicken is deep-fried. In this version, boneless chicken thighs and lots of vegetables are smothered in an easy and delicious orange sauce. I cook a bowl of jasmine rice in the same pot for serving, but you could also serve this with Easy Cauliflower "Rice" (page 56) for a low-carb alternative.

1. Combine the orange juice and zest, maple syrup, soy sauce, vinegar, ginger, garlic, and red pepper flakes in the Instant Pot and stir well. Place the chicken thighs on top of the sauce. Arrange a 2.5-inch trivet (see page 12) over the chicken and place a 7-inch oven-safe bowl on top. Add the rice and 1 cup of the water to the bowl. Secure the lid and move the steam release valve to **Sealing**. Select **Manual/Pressure Cook** to cook on high pressure for 12 minutes.

2. When the cooking cycle is complete, quickly release the pressure by moving the steam release valve to **Venting**. When the floating valve drops, remove the lid and press **Cancel**. Use oven mitts to lift the trivet and the bowl out of the pot. Fluff the rice with a fork. Use tongs to transfer the chicken to a cutting board.

3. Press **Sauté** and add the onion, bell pepper, and broccoli. Stir well and simmer until the vegetables are fork-tender, about 8 minutes. In a small bowl, stir together the arrowroot and the remaining 2 tablespoons water to make a slurry.

4. While the vegetables are cooking, cut the chicken into bite-sized chunks and stir them into the simmering sauce. Add the slurry to the pot and stir well. The sauce will thicken and become glossy within 1 to 2 minutes. Serve the orange chicken warm over the rice with green onion and sesame seeds sprinkled on top. Store leftovers in an airtight container in the fridge for 3 or 4 days.

MAKE IT VEGAN Omit the chicken, and use green lentils instead. Because the lentils won't become tender if you cook them in the sauce, you have to cook them first. Add 1 cup green lentils and 1¼ cups water to the Instant Pot. Arrange the trivet on top of the lentils and add the rice as instructed. Cook on high pressure for 5 minutes, then let the pressure naturally release for 10 minutes. Add the sauce and vegetables and simmer as directed.

MAKE IT GLUTEN-FREE Use tamari instead of soy sauce.

Per Serving (with rice): Calories 388, Fat 5g, Carbohydrates 58g, Fiber 4g, Protein 28g

Coconut-Lime Shrimp

This easy weeknight shrimp dish features a perfect combination of creamy coconut and tart lime. Served with cauliflower "rice," which conveniently cooks in the same pot, it's a low-carb meal with plenty of veggies to keep you feeling satisfied. A word of caution: don't be tempted to pressure cook the shrimp as it will end up with a rubbery texture. Luckily, the shrimp cooks in just minutes using the Instant Pot's sauté function.

1. Combine the coconut milk, lime juice, Sriracha, bell pepper, salt, and several grinds of pepper in the Instant Pot.

2. Arrange a steamer basket over the sauce in the bottom of the pot and place the cauliflower in the basket. Secure the lid and move the steam release valve to **Sealing**. Select **Manual/Pressure Cook** to cook on high pressure for 1 minute.

3. When the cooking cycle is complete, quickly release the pressure by moving the steam release valve to **Venting**. When the floating valve drops, remove the lid and press **Cancel** to stop the cooking cycle.

4. Use oven mitts to lift the steamer basket of cauliflower out of the pot. Press **Sauté** and add the shrimp and snap peas to the pot. Stir well, simmering the shrimp in the sauce until they are cooked through with a pink exterior, about 3 minutes for fresh and 5 to 6 minutes for frozen.

5. Transfer the cooked cauliflower to a large bowl and use a potato masher to break up the florets into ricelike pieces.

6. Add the cilantro to the pot, then ladle the shrimp and vegetables over the cauliflower "rice." Serve with lime wedges on the side.

MAKE IT VEGAN Omit the shrimp and use 3 cups cooked white beans instead (two 15-ounce cans, drained and rinsed). Cook the beans and the snap peas, with the cauliflower basket on top of them, on high pressure for just 1 minute, then quickly release the pressure so the vegetables don't overcook.

Per Serving: Calories 259, Fat 11g, Carbohydrates 16g, Fiber 5g, Protein 20g

SERVES 4

Prep: 10 minutes
Pressurize: 6 minutes
Cook: 4 to 7 minutes
Quick Release
Total: 20 to 23 minutes

1 cup full-fat coconut milk (see page 8)

2 tablespoons freshly squeezed lime juice

1 tablespoon Sriracha

1 red bell pepper, seeded and chopped

½ teaspoon fine sea salt

Freshly ground black pepper

1 small head cauliflower, cut into florets (about 8 ounces)

1 pound fresh or frozen raw shrimp, peeled and deveined

8 ounces sugar snap peas

½ cup lightly packed chopped fresh cilantro

Lime wedges, for serving

Carolina Barbecued Chicken
with Simple Slaw

SERVES 4

Prep: 10 minutes
Pressurize: 6 minutes
Cook: 20 minutes
Quick Release
Total: 36 minutes

BARBECUED CHICKEN

½ yellow onion, chopped

1 clove garlic, minced

¼ cup raw apple cider vinegar

¼ cup pure maple syrup (see page 10)

¼ cup water

1 tablespoon soy sauce or tamari

1 pound boneless, skinless chicken breasts

1 teaspoon fine sea salt

Freshly ground black pepper

¼ cup tomato paste

1 teaspoon blackstrap molasses

1 teaspoon spicy brown mustard

½ teaspoon chili powder

½ teaspoon paprika

⅛ teaspoon cayenne pepper (optional)

¼ head green cabbage, shredded (about 8 ounces)

This quick homemade barbecue sauce is simmered with shredded cabbage, which becomes almost undetectable when paired with shredded chicken. It's a nice way to increase your vegetable intake without much effort. Serve this tangy chicken with the crunchy slaw on top for a nice contrast of flavors and textures.

1. To make the barbecued chicken, add the onion, garlic, vinegar, maple syrup, water, and soy sauce to the Instant Pot and stir to combine. Arrange the handled trivet (see page 11) in the bottom of the pot and place the chicken breasts on top. Season the breasts with ¼ teaspoon of the salt and several grinds of black pepper. Secure the lid and move the steam release valve to **Sealing.** Select **Manual/Pressure Cook** to cook on high pressure for 12 minutes.

2. While the chicken is cooking, prepare the slaw (see page 163). In a large bowl, combine the lemon juice, maple syrup, olive oil, salt, and several grinds of pepper and stir well. Add the cabbage, carrot, and parsley and toss to coat. Refrigerate the slaw to let the flavors meld while you finish preparing the chicken.

3. When the cooking cycle is complete, quickly release the pressure by moving the steam release valve to **Venting**. When the floating valve drops, remove the lid. Press **Cancel** and use tongs to transfer the chicken to a cutting board to rest. Use oven mitts to remove the trivet.

4. Press **Sauté** and add the tomato paste, molasses, mustard, chili powder, paprika, cayenne, and the remaining ¾ teaspoon salt to the sauce. Stir well, then add the cabbage. Simmer the cabbage in the sauce until very tender, about 8 minutes.

5. Once the cabbage is tender, use two forks to shred the chicken. Add it to the pot and stir well. Taste and adjust the seasonings as needed; add more cayenne if you like it spicy.

6. To serve, scoop the barbecued chicken into lettuce cups or onto your favorite buns, with the chilled slaw on top. Serve any additional slaw on the side. Store leftovers in two separate airtight containers in the fridge. The chicken will keep for 3 or 4 days, but the slaw is best used within 1 day.

CONTINUED

MAKE IT VEGAN Omit the chicken and use green jackfruit instead. Jackfruit is a large tropical fruit with a green outer skin and a tender inside with a similar texture to artichoke hearts. It's commonly sold in cans, so you just drain and rinse it to use in recipes that require a shredded texture, such as replacing pulled pork or shredded chicken.

Drain and rinse one 20-ounce can green jackfruit to remove the salty brine, then use your hands or two forks to shred it as you would cooked chicken. Add the jackfruit to the pot along with the rest of the sauce ingredients, and use only ½ teaspoon salt. Select **Manual/Pressure Cook** to cook on high pressure for 3 minutes. When the cooking cycle is complete, immediately move the steam release valve to **Venting** to quickly release the steam pressure. When the floating valve drops, remove the lid, stir in the cabbage, and simmer as instructed. Taste and adjust the seasonings as needed, adding more salt or maple syrup.

MAKE IT GLUTEN-FREE Use tamari instead of soy sauce.

Per Serving (without buns): Calories 320, Fat 10g, Carbohydrates 29g, Fiber 4g, Protein 24g

SIMPLE SLAW

2 tablespoons freshly squeezed lemon juice

2 tablespoons pure maple syrup (see page 10)

1 tablespoon extra-virgin olive oil

½ teaspoon fine sea salt

Freshly ground black pepper

¼ head green cabbage, shredded (about 8 ounces)

1 cup shredded carrot (about 1 large carrot)

¼ cup chopped fresh flat-leaf parsley

Butter lettuce or buns, for serving

Chicken Tikka Masala

SERVES 6

Prep: 10 minutes
Pressurize: 10 to 15 minutes
Cook: 13 minutes
Quick Release
Total: 33 to 38 minutes

1 yellow onion, chopped

One 28-ounce can diced tomatoes (see page 10)

1 teaspoon garam masala

1 teaspoon ground cumin

1 tablespoon ground coriander

1 teaspoon paprika

¼ teaspoon ground cinnamon

¼ teaspoon ground ginger

¼ teaspoon cayenne pepper (optional)

1 tablespoon pure maple syrup (see page 10)

1½ pounds boneless, skinless chicken thighs

2 teaspoons fine sea salt

1 cup long-grain white rice, like jasmine or basmati

1¼ cups water

½ head cauliflower, chopped (about 1 pound)

1½ cups peeled, chopped carrots (about 3 carrots)

½ cup full-fat canned coconut milk (see page 8)

This popular Indian dish is typically made with heavy cream and few vegetables, so I've given it a nutrient upgrade with more than a pound of cauliflower and carrots. The resulting meal may not be quite as authentic, but I love how the vegetables become nearly undetectable in this rich sauce. I serve it with naan, and use coconut milk to give it a dairy-free creaminess, but you could leave it out for less fat and a richer tomato flavor.

1. Combine the onion, tomatoes with their juices, garam masala, cumin, coriander, paprika, cinnamon, ginger, cayenne, and maple syrup in the Instant Pot and use an immersion blender to blend until smooth. (Alternatively, place the ingredients in a blender and blend until smooth, then pour the sauce into the pot.) Place the chicken on top of the sauce and season it with the salt.

2. Arrange a 2.5-inch trivet (see page 12) over the chicken and place a 7-inch oven-safe bowl on top. Add the rice and water to the bowl. Secure the lid and move the steam release valve to **Sealing**. Select **Manual/Pressure Cook** to cook on high pressure for 12 minutes. When the cooking cycle is complete, immediately move the steam release valve to **Venting** to quickly release the steam pressure. When the floating valve drops, remove the lid.

3. Use oven mitts to lift the trivet and the bowl of cooked rice out of the pot. Fluff the rice with a fork. Use tongs to transfer the cooked chicken to a cutting board. Add the cauliflower and carrots to the sauce. Secure the lid and move the steam release valve to **Sealing**. Select **Manual/Pressure Cook** to cook on high pressure for 1 minute. When the cooking cycle is complete, immediately move the steam release valve to **Venting** to quickly release the steam pressure. When the floating valve drops, remove the lid.

4. Cut the chicken into bite-sized pieces and stir them into the sauce. Stir in the coconut milk, then taste and adjust the seasonings as needed. Serve warm over the rice. Store leftovers in an airtight container in the fridge for 3 or 4 days.

MAKE IT VEGAN Omit the chicken and instead add 3 cups cooked chickpeas or two 15-ounce cans rinsed and drained chickpeas. Decrease the salt to 1 teaspoon and cook on high pressure for only 4 minutes. Let the pressure naturally release for 10 minutes to finish cooking the rice, then add the cauliflower and carrots as instructed.

Per Serving: Calories 291, Fat 8g, Carbohydrates 29g, Fiber 4g, Protein 26g

Creamy Chicken & Brown Rice

Chicken and rice is a classic comfort food combination. This recipe is healthier and tastier than the original, forgoing the canned soup and using brown rice instead of white rice to boost the fiber content.

1. Press **Sauté** and add the olive oil to the Instant Pot. Once the oil is hot but not smoking, add the onion, mushrooms, and garlic and sauté until softened, about 5 minutes.

2. Add the brown rice, water, thyme, and ½ teaspoon of the salt and stir well, scraping the bottom of the pot with a wooden spoon or spatula to make sure nothing has stuck. Place the chicken breasts on top of the rice mixture and season with the remaining ½ teaspoon salt and several grinds of pepper. Press **Cancel**, then secure the lid and move the steam release valve to **Sealing**. Select **Manual/Pressure Cook** to cook on high pressure for 10 minutes.

3. When the cooking cycle is complete, quickly release the pressure by moving the steam release valve to **Venting**. When the floating valve drops, remove the lid and use tongs to transfer the chicken to a cutting board to rest for 5 minutes. If using fresh peas, add them now, scattering them over the rice. Secure the lid again, making sure the sealing ring is properly placed. Move the steam release valve to **Sealing** and select **Manual/Pressure Cook** to cook on high pressure for 8 minutes more. While the rice cooks, cut the chicken into bite-sized pieces.

4. When the cooking cycle is complete, let the pressure naturally release for 10 minutes, then move the steam release valve to **Venting**. When the floating valve drops, remove the lid and stir the chicken into the rice, along with the lemon juice and coconut milk. If using frozen peas, add them now. Taste and adjust the seasoning as needed, then serve immediately. Store leftovers in an airtight container in the fridge for 3 or 4 days.

MAKE IT VEGAN Omit the chicken and salt in step 2 and instead add 1 cup (unsoaked) dried navy beans and increase the water to 2¼ cups. Cook on high pressure for 22 minutes, then let the pressure naturally release for 10 minutes. Season with 1 teaspoon salt when you add the frozen peas, lemon juice, and coconut milk.

SERVES 4

Prep: 5 minutes
Pressurize: 5 minutes
Cook: 23 minutes
Natural Release: 10 minutes
Total: 43 minutes

1 tablespoon extra-virgin olive oil

1 yellow onion, chopped

8 ounces cremini mushrooms, roughly chopped

2 cloves garlic, minced

1 cup long-grain brown rice, rinsed

1¼ cups water

1 teaspoon dried thyme

1 teaspoon fine sea salt

1 pound boneless, skinless chicken breasts

Freshly ground black pepper

1 cup fresh or frozen peas

1 tablespoon freshly squeezed lemon juice

¼ cup full-fat canned coconut milk (see page 8)

Per Serving: Calories 390, Fat 9g, Carbohydrates 50g, Fiber 6g, Protein 32g

Sneaky Sloppy Joes

SERVES 4

Prep: 5 minutes
Pressurize: 10 minutes
Cook: 28 minutes
Natural Release:
10 minutes
Total: 53 minutes

1 tablespoon extra-virgin olive oil

1 yellow onion, chopped

1 pound ground turkey

1 teaspoon chili powder

1½ teaspoons fine sea salt

½ cup water

1 green bell pepper, seeded and chopped

½ cup tomato paste (about 6 ounces)

1 butternut squash (about 1 pound), peeled and cut into 1-inch cubes, or 8 ounces frozen butternut squash pieces

2 tablespoons pure maple syrup (see page 10)

1½ tablespoons spicy brown mustard

Freshly ground black pepper

2 small sweet potatoes (each 11 ounces or less; see Note), pierced with a fork to vent

Chopped green onions, tender white and green parts only, for garnish

Chopped fresh flat-leaf parsley, for garnish

Sloppy joes is a classic childhood favorite. This version sneaks a serving of butternut squash into the filling. The squash dissolves when cooked under pressure and naturally thickens the sauce. I pack the filling into baked sweet potatoes, which are cooked at the same time for an easy one-pot meal.

1. Press **Sauté** and add the olive oil to the Instant Pot. Once the oil is hot but not smoking, add the onion, turkey, chili powder, and 1 teaspoon of the salt and sauté until the turkey is browned and cooked through, breaking it up with a wooden spoon as you stir, about 8 minutes. Press **Cancel** to stop the cooking cycle.

2. Add the water and scrape up anything that has stuck to the bottom of the pot. Without stirring, add the bell pepper, tomato paste, butternut squash cubes, maple syrup, mustard, remaining ½ teaspoon salt, and several grinds of pepper.

3. Arrange a 4-inch trivet (see page 12) on top of the filling and place the sweet potatoes on the trivet. Secure the lid and move the steam release valve to **Sealing**. Select **Manual/Pressure Cook** to cook on high pressure for 20 minutes.

4. When the cooking cycle is complete, let the pressure naturally release for 10 minutes, then move the steam release valve to **Venting** to release any remaining pressure. When the floating valve drops, remove the lid. Use oven mitts to lift the trivet and potatoes out of the pot. Stir the filling, using a wooden spoon to mash up the squash. Press **Sauté** to simmer away excess liquid until the sauce is to your liking. Adjust the seasoning as needed.

5. Carefully slice the hot sweet potatoes in half lengthwise and spoon filling over each half. Garnish with the green onions and parsley and serve immediately. Store leftover filling in an airtight container in the fridge for 3 or 4 days.

MAKE IT VEGAN Omit the turkey and salt in step 1, and sauté for only 5 minutes. Omit the mustard in step 2, increase the water to 1½ cups total, and add 1 cup green lentils to the pot. Cook as instructed, then add 1½ teaspoons salt to the lentils once tender. Stir in the mustard and serve warm.

NOTE If your potatoes are larger than 11 ounces, roast in a 400°F oven until tender, 45 to 60 minutes. Shorten the pressure cooking time by 10 minutes to cook the sauce.

Per Serving: Calories 380, Fat 12g, Carbohydrates 46g, Fiber 8g, Protein 27g

CHAPTER
7

Naturally
Sweet Treats

Fresh Apple Crumble

If you love apple pie, you'll love this easy hands–off dessert. I top freshly chopped apples with a buttery oat and cinnamon crumble for apple pie flavor without the effort. Serve this with ice cream, or on its own, for a fiber-rich treat.

1. Add the apples and the water to the Instant Pot and stir well to be sure the apples cover the bottom of the pot in an even layer.

2. In a separate bowl, combine the flour, oats, coconut sugar, cinnamon, and salt and stir well. Add the melted coconut oil and stir until thoroughly mixed.

3. Spoon the oat crumble over the apples as a topping. Secure the lid and move the steam release valve to **Sealing**. Select **Manual/Pressure Cook** to cook on high pressure for 8 minutes.

4. When the cooking cycle is complete, let the pressure naturally release for 10 minutes, then move the steam release valve to **Venting** to release any remaining pressure. When the floating valve drops, remove the lid.

5. Use oven mitts to remove the insert from the Instant Pot and let the crumble cool for 10 minutes before serving warm. This dessert has the best taste and texture when it's served the day it is made, so I don't recommend making it ahead of time for guests. Store leftovers in an airtight container in the fridge for 5 days.

MAKE IT GLUTEN-FREE Replace the whole-wheat flour with ¼ cup certified gluten-free oat flour. If you can't find it, make your own by grinding certified gluten-free rolled oats in a coffee grinder or blender until the texture is very fine and no whole oats remain.

NOTE I don't recommend making fruit substitutions with this recipe. I tested it with frozen berries and peaches, but the crumble topping completely dissolved into the fruit. Fresh fruit seems to work best in this case.

Per Serving: Calories 279, Fat 10g, Carbohydrates 48g, Fiber 7g, Protein 2g

Prep: 15 minutes
Pressurize: 7 minutes
Cook: 8 minutes
Natural Release: 10 minutes
Total: 40 minutes, plus cooling

5 large apples (about 2 pounds), cut into 1-inch chunks

⅓ cup water

3 tablespoons 100 percent white whole-wheat flour (see page 11)

¾ cup quick-cooking oats

½ cup coconut sugar

2 teaspoons ground cinnamon

¼ teaspoon fine sea salt

¼ cup melted coconut oil or butter

Flourless Brownies

These brownies are lower in sugar and fat than traditional brownies, but they still taste decadent enough to satisfy a sweet tooth. Baking in the Instant Pot keeps the brownies moist, with no risk of overbaking. Don't be alarmed by the thickness of the batter, or by how soft the brownies might look immediately after cooking. They firm up as they cool, with a perfectly fudgy texture. I like to splurge and use dark chocolate chips for added texture in these naturally sweetened brownies, but you can leave them out completely to avoid the refined sugar.

1. Line a 7-inch round pan with parchment paper. In a large bowl, combine the almond butter, coconut sugar, cacao powder, egg, salt, baking soda, and vanilla and stir well to create a thick batter.

2. Transfer the batter to the prepared pan and use your hands to press it evenly into the pan. Sprinkle with the chocolate chips and gently press them into the batter. Pour 1 cup water into the Instant Pot and arrange the handled trivet (see page 11) on the bottom. Place the pan on top of the trivet and cover it with an upside-down plate or another piece of parchment to protect the brownies from condensation.

3. Secure the lid and move the steam release valve to **Sealing**. Select **Manual/Pressure Cook** to cook on high pressure for 15 minutes. When the cooking cycle is complete, let the pressure naturally release for 10 minutes, then move the steam release valve to **Venting** to release any remaining pressure. When the floating valve drops, remove the lid.

4. Use oven mitts to lift the trivet and the pan out of the pot. Let the brownies cool completely in the pan before cutting and serving, as they will be very fragile when warm. Store leftovers in an airtight container in the fridge for 2 weeks.

MAKE IT VEGAN Omit the egg and instead combine 1 tablespoon ground flax or chia seeds with 3 tablespoons water for an egg substitute. Add 1 teaspoon raw apple cider vinegar to help the "egg" react with the baking soda. Add 10 minutes to the pressure cooking time, then follow the instructions as given.

Per Brownie: Calories 125, Fat 7g, Carbohydrates 12g, Fiber 2g, Protein 3g

---

MAKES 16

Prep: 10 minutes
Pressurize: 10 minutes
Cook: 15 minutes
Natural Release: 10 minutes
Total: 45 minutes, plus cooling

¾ cup almond butter

¾ cup coconut sugar

⅓ cup raw cacao powder

1 egg

¼ teaspoon fine sea salt

½ teaspoon baking soda

½ teaspoon pure vanilla extract

½ cup dark chocolate chips (optional)

Brown Rice Pudding

SERVES 6

Prep: 5 minutes
Pressurize: 10 minutes
Cook: 22 minutes
Natural Release:
10 minutes
Total: 47 minutes

1 cup long-grain brown rice, like jasmine or basmati, rinsed

2 cups water

One 15-ounce can full-fat coconut milk (see page 8)

⅓ cup maple syrup (see page 10)

½ teaspoon pure vanilla extract

½ teaspoon ground cinnamon, plus more for serving

Pinch of fine sea salt

If you love rice pudding, you'll love this dairy-free and naturally sweetened version. Making it with brown rice boosts the fiber content, so it won't drastically spike your blood sugar, and briefly pulsing it with an immersion blender gives it a similar creaminess to the traditional version made with white rice. Use full-fat canned coconut milk for the creamiest results, or use light canned coconut milk to lower the fat and calorie content even more. Top with your favorite chopped fruit and nuts.

1. Combine the rice and water in the bottom of the Instant Pot and secure the lid, moving the steam release valve to **Sealing**. Select **Manual/Pressure Cook** to cook on high pressure for 22 minutes.

2. When the cooking cycle has completed, allow the pressure to naturally release for 10 minutes before moving the steam release valve to **Venting**. Carefully remove the lid.

3. Stir the rice, making sure that it's tender, then add in the coconut milk, maple syrup, vanilla, cinnamon, and salt. Stir well to combine and adjust any seasoning to taste.

4. Use an immersion blender directly in the pot to briefly pulse the pudding until your desired texture has been reached. The more you blend, the creamier it will be. Serve warm, with extra cinnamon on top. If you'd prefer to serve it cold, transfer it to an airtight container and chill for 2 hours. The pudding will thicken and you'll need to add water to thin it to your desired serving consistency again. (I'd start with ½ cup water and add more as needed.) Store leftovers in an airtight container in the fridge for 4 days.

Per Serving: Calories 260, Fat 12g, Carbohydrates 39g, Fiber 2g, Protein 3g

Cinnamon-Pecan Coffee Cake

This nutty coffee cake made with naturally gluten-free almond flour will keep you feeling satisfied all morning. Almond *flour* is typically made from ground blanched almonds, but you could also use almond *meal*, which includes the skins, for a slightly denser cake. Taking into account the eggs and the low-glycemic coconut sugar, this cake should help your blood sugar levels stay balanced, making it a relatively healthy brunch or dessert option.

SERVES 8

Prep: 10 minutes
Pressurize: 6 minutes
Cook: 30 minutes
Natural Release: 10 minutes
Total: 56 minutes, plus cooling

1½ cups almond flour or almond meal

¾ cup coconut sugar

½ teaspoon baking soda

¼ teaspoon fine sea salt

1 teaspoon ground cinnamon

3 eggs, at room temperature

2 tablespoons melted coconut oil

½ cup finely chopped pecans

1. Lightly grease a 7-inch round pan and line it with parchment paper. In a large bowl, combine the almond flour, coconut sugar, baking soda, salt, and cinnamon and whisk to break up any lumps. Add the eggs and melted coconut oil and mix with a spatula until smooth. (If your eggs are cold from the fridge, the mixture will be thick and difficult to stir, but the cake will still bake well.) Pour the batter into the pan and smooth the top with the spatula. Sprinkle the pecans over the batter.

2. Pour 1 cup water into the Instant Pot and arrange the handled trivet (see page 11) on the bottom. Place the pan on top of the trivet and cover it with an upside-down plate or another piece of parchment to protect the cake from condensation. Secure the lid and move the steam release valve to **Sealing**. Select **Manual/Pressure Cook** to cook on high pressure for 30 minutes.

3. When the cooking cycle is complete, let the pressure naturally release for 10 minutes, then move the steam release valve to **Venting** to release any remaining pressure. When the floating valve drops, remove the lid. Use oven mitts to lift the trivet and the pan out of the pot. Let the cake cool in the pan for 30 minutes before cutting and serving. Store leftovers in an airtight container in the fridge for 1 week.

MAKE IT VEGAN Replace the almond flour with 1⅓ cups oat flour, omit the eggs, and add 1 tablespoon ground flax or chia seeds, ¼ cup warm water, and 1 teaspoon raw apple cider vinegar to the batter. Cook for 40 minutes at high pressure and release as directed.

Per Serving: Calories 202, Fat 13g, Carbohydrates 20g, Fiber 1g, Protein 4g

Creamy Coconut-Ginger Pudding

SERVES 4

Prep: 5 minutes
Pressurize: 6 minutes
Cook: 10 minutes
Quick Release
Total: 21 minutes

1 large sweet potato (about 1 pound), peeled and cut into 1-inch pieces

½ cup full-fat canned coconut milk (see page 8)

6 tablespoons pure maple syrup (see page 10), plus more as needed

1 teaspoon grated fresh ginger (about ½-inch knob), plus more as needed

This creamy pudding is made from ultra-tender sweet potatoes, which blend easily when cooked in the Instant Pot. I flavor this pudding with creamy coconut milk and freshly grated ginger, but you could also add raw cacao powder or vanilla to change it up. Sweet potatoes come in different varieties, including the classic orange jewel, white Hannah, and purple Japanese varieties. If you can find the purple ones, the pudding is a fun and colorful treat for kids.

1. Pour 1 cup water into the Instant Pot and arrange a steamer basket on the bottom. Place the sweet potato pieces in the steamer basket and secure the lid, moving the steam release valve to **Sealing**. Select **Manual/Pressure Cook** to cook on high pressure for 10 minutes. When the cooking cycle is complete, immediately move the steam release valve to **Venting** to quickly release the steam pressure. When the floating valve drops, remove the lid.

2. Use oven mitts to lift the steamer basket out of the pot and transfer the cooked potatoes to a large bowl. Add the coconut milk, maple syrup, and ginger. Use an immersion blender or potato masher to puree the potatoes into a smooth pudding. Taste and adjust the flavor, adding more ginger or maple syrup as needed.

3. Serve the pudding right away, or chill it in the fridge. (Cold pudding will have a slightly muted flavor, so keep that in mind as you adjust the ginger and maple syrup.) Store leftover pudding in an airtight container in the fridge for 1 week.

Per Serving: Calories 181, Fat 2g, Carbohydrates 43g, Fiber 4g, Protein 2g

Deep-Dish Oatmeal Raisin Cookie

I love making desserts in the Instant Pot because there's no risk of burning them in the oven, and you also avoid heating up your entire kitchen in the process. This is a decadent treat that cooks to perfection while you do other things around the house. Though it's hard to resist, be sure to let this cookie cool completely before digging in, for best flavor and texture.

1. Grease a 7-inch round pan and line it with parchment paper. In a large bowl, stir together the flour, sugar, salt, baking soda, and cinnamon. Add the egg, coconut oil, and vanilla and stir until a smooth batter forms. Fold in the oats and raisins. The batter will be thick and sticky. Transfer the batter to the prepared pan and use a spatula to smooth the top.

2. Pour 1 cup water into the Instant Pot and arrange the handled trivet (see page 11) on the bottom. Place the pan on top of the trivet and cover it with an upside-down plate or another piece of parchment to protect the cookie from condensation. Secure the lid and move the steam release valve to **Sealing**. Select **Manual/Pressure Cook** to cook on high pressure for 25 minutes.

3. When the cooking cycle is complete, let the pressure naturally release for 10 minutes, then move the steam release valve to **Venting** to release any remaining pressure. When the floating valve drops, remove the lid. Use oven mitts to lift the trivet and the pan out of the pot. Let the cookie cool completely, about 1 hour, before cutting and serving. Store leftovers in an airtight container in the fridge for 1 week.

MAKE IT VEGAN Omit the egg and instead combine 1 tablespoon ground flax or chia seeds with 3 tablespoons water for an egg substitute. Add 1 teaspoon raw apple cider vinegar to help the "egg" react with the baking soda. Follow the instructions as given.

MAKE IT GLUTEN-FREE Replace the whole-wheat flour with ½ cup certified gluten-free oat flour.

Per Serving: Calories 218, Fat 8g, Carbohydrates 34g, Fiber 4g, Protein 4g

SERVES 8

Prep: 10 minutes
Pressurize: 5 minutes
Cook: 25 minutes
Natural Release: 10 minutes
Total: 50 minutes, plus cooling

½ cup 100 percent white whole-wheat flour (see page 11)

½ cup coconut sugar

¼ teaspoon fine sea salt

¼ teaspoon baking soda

1 teaspoon ground cinnamon

1 egg

¼ cup melted coconut oil or butter

½ teaspoon pure vanilla extract

½ cup quick-cooking oats

½ cup raisins

One-Pot Chocolate Cake with Chocolate Frosting

MAKES 1 SINGLE-LAYER 7-INCH CAKE; SERVES 6 TO 8

Prep: 20 minutes
Pressurize: 5 minutes
Cook: 40 minutes
Natural Release: 10 minutes
Total: 1 hour 15 minutes, plus cooling

CHOCOLATE FROSTING

1 cup water

½ sweet potato (about 8 ounces), peeled and cut into chunks

3 tablespoons raw cacao powder

6 tablespoons pure maple syrup (see page 10)

1 tablespoon melted coconut oil or butter

½ teaspoon pure vanilla extract

Pinch of fine sea salt

CHOCOLATE CAKE

½ cup 100 percent white whole-wheat flour (see page 11)

5 tablespoons raw cacao powder

1 cup coconut sugar

½ teaspoon baking soda

¼ teaspoon fine sea salt

2 eggs, at room temperature

¼ cup melted coconut oil or butter

2 tablespoons water

This moist chocolate cake is a one-pot wonder because the cake and frosting are both prepared in the same pot at the same time. Sweet potatoes make a creamy, low-fat base for the frosting, but no one will know your secret thanks to its rich chocolate flavor.

1. To make the frosting, pour the water into the Instant Pot and place the sweet potato chunks in the bottom. Arrange a 2.5-inch trivet (see page 12) over the potatoes.

2. To make the cake, grease a 7-inch round pan with coconut oil or butter and press a piece of parchment paper into the bottom. In a large bowl, whisk together the flour, cacao powder, coconut sugar, baking soda, and salt, breaking up any large clumps. Add the eggs, coconut oil, and water and whisk again, until a uniform batter forms. (If your eggs are cold from the fridge, the batter will be thick and difficult to stir, but the cake will still bake well.) Pour the batter into the pan and use a spatula to smooth the top.

3. Place the cake pan on top of the trivet and cover it with an upside-down plate or another piece of parchment to protect the cake from condensation. Secure the lid and move the steam release valve to **Sealing**. Select **Manual/Pressure Cook** to cook on high pressure for 40 minutes. When the cooking cycle is complete, let the pressure naturally release for 10 minutes, then move the steam release valve to **Venting** to release any remaining pressure. When the floating valve drops, remove the lid.

4. Use oven mitts to lift the trivet and the cake pan out of the pot. Let the cake cool completely in the pan, about 1 hour. (You can speed up the process by chilling it in the fridge.)

5. To finish the frosting, drain the cooked sweet potatoes through a colander and transfer them to a mixing bowl. Use an immersion blender or potato masher to puree the potatoes until smooth. Add the cacao powder, maple syrup, coconut oil, vanilla, and salt and whisk to combine. The frosting will become silky smooth. Taste and adjust the flavor, adding more cacao powder or maple syrup as needed. Chill the frosting in the fridge for 1 hour. It will thicken as it cools.

CONTINUED

6. Once the cake and frosting have cooled completely, frost the cake and slice to serve. Store leftovers in an airtight container in the fridge for 1 week.

FOR A TWO-LAYER CAKE Double the recipe and stack a second 7-inch pan on top of the first one to cook both layers at once without adjusting the cook time. If using a 6-quart Instant Pot, stack the handled trivet directly on top of the sweet potatoes (instead of using a 2.5-inch trivet) so the stacked pans fit.

MAKE IT VEGAN For the cake, replace the whole-wheat flour with 1 cup certified gluten-free oat flour. Omit the eggs and increase the water to ¼ cup total, add 1 tablespoon ground flax or chia seeds and 1 teaspoon raw apple cider vinegar. This version will be denser than the original recipe, but still delicious!

MAKE IT GLUTEN-FREE Replace the whole-wheat flour with ¾ cup certified gluten-free oat flour. The vegan option above is also gluten-free.

Per Serving: Calories 298, Fat 10g, Carbohydrates 49g, Fiber 3g, Protein 4g

Pressure Cooking Time Charts

If you want to experiment with ingredients not included in the recipes in this book, the following time charts will help you get started. There are many variables that can affect timing, including size, weight, seasonings, and altitude, so consider these recommendations as a general starting point.

Beans and Legumes

See page 68 for soaking information and cooking instructions. If you don't have time to soak your beans, use the unsoaked cooking times below. For every 1 cup of beans, use 1 cup of water for soaked beans and 2 cups of water for dried beans. Use 1½ cups of water for every 1 cup of lentils.

BEANS AND LEGUMES	MINUTES AT HIGH PRESSURE, SOAKED	MINUTES AT HIGH PRESSURE, UNSOAKED	RELEASE
Adzuki	4–6	16–20	15 minutes
Black Beans	10–15	22–30	15 minutes
Black-Eyed Peas	5–10	10–15	15 minutes
Cannelini Beans	10–15	30–35	15 minutes
Chickpeas (Garbanzo Beans)	12–15	45–60	15 minutes
Great Northern Beans	7–8	25–30	15 minutes
Kidney Beans	10–15	25–30	15 minutes
Lentils, brown or green**	——	4–5	10 minutes
Lentils, red**	——	3	5 minutes
Lima Beans	3–6	12–14	15 minutes
Navy Beans	10–15	20–25	15 minutes
Pinto Beans	10–15	25–30	15 minutes
Soybeans	18–20	35–45	15 minutes
Split Peas	——	5–10	10 minutes

Grains and Pasta

Because there is no evaporation in the Instant Pot, you need less cooking liquid to prepare grains than when using a stove top. Unless a different release time is noted in the chart below, let the pressure naturally release for 10 minutes, then move the steam release valve to Venting to release any remaining pressure. When the floating valve drops, remove the lid.

When cooking rice, be sure to rinse it before cooking to help remove debris and surface starch. This prevents the rice from clumping together or developing a gummy texture. To reduce phytic acid and boost mineral absorption, try soaking brown rice in water for up to 24 hours in the fridge and then drain and rinse it before cooking as directed.

GRAINS AND PASTA	LIQUID PER CUP	MINUTES AT HIGH PRESSURE	RELEASE
Amaranth*	1 cup	5	10 minutes
Barley, pearled	1¼ cups	20	10 minutes
Brown Rice, long-grain*	1 cup	22	10 minutes
Bulgur	1¼ cups	1	10 minutes
Couscous, whole-wheat	1¼ cups	1	10 minutes
Farro	1 cup	10	10 minutes
Gluten-Free Pasta*	3 cups	0	8 minutes
Kamut	1½ cups	10	10 minutes
Millet*	1½ cups	5	10 minutes
Oats, rolled**	1½ cups	3	10 minutes
Oats, steel-cut**	2 cups	4	10 minutes
Quinoa*	1 cup	1	10 minutes
Sorghum	1½ cups	22	10 minutes
Spelt Berries	1 cup	25	10 minutes
Wheat Berries	1½ cups	25	10 minutes
White Rice, short-grain*	1 cup	4	10 minutes
White Rice, long-grain*	1 cup	4	10 minutes
Whole-Wheat Pasta	4 cups	3–4	10 minutes
Wild Rice*	1½ cups	25	10 minutes

* Gluten-free   ** Gluten-free, but due to the possibility of cross-contamination during manufacturing, look for versions labeled "certified gluten-free."

Meat, Poultry, and Fish

Below are general cooking times, but sticking to a recipe that gives exact cooking times ensures you don't overcook or undercook your meat, poultry, or fish.

MEAT, POULTRY, AND FISH	MINUTES AT HIGH PRESSURE	RELEASE
Beef Brisket	60–90 (20 min. per pound)	10 minutes
Beef, ground	8–10	10 minutes
Chicken Breasts, bone-in	7–10 (8 min. per pound)	10 minutes
Chicken Breasts, boneless	4	10 minutes
Chicken Breasts, frozen	12–20	10 minutes
Chicken Thighs, bone-in	12–15	10 minutes
Chicken Thighs, boneless	10–12	5 minutes
Cod	2–3	Quick
Duck Quarters, bone-in	10–12	10 minutes
Pork Chops	6–10	10 minutes
Pork Shoulder	45–60 (20 min. per pound)	10 minutes
Pot Roast	40–70	10 minutes
Salmon	2–3	Quick
Turkey Breast, boneless	15–20	10 minutes
Turkey, ground	8–10	Quick or 10 minutes

Vegetables

Vegetables cook very quickly in the Instant Pot. Pour 1 cup water into the pot and place the vegetables in a steamer basket about 1 inch above the water. (You can also cook the vegetables in a bowl placed on the handled trivet, but the cooking times will be longer.)

Stay close to the device to hear the beep when it goes off. When the cooking cycle is complete, immediately move the steam release valve to Venting to quickly release the steam pressure. When the floating valve drops, remove the lid.

VEGETABLES	MINUTES AT HIGH PRESSURE	RELEASE
Artichokes	8–10	Quick
Beets, whole	15–20	Quick
Broccoli, cut into florets	0–1	Quick
Brussels Sprouts, whole	2–3	Quick
Butternut Squash, cut into 1-inch chunks	4	Quick
Cabbage, shredded	0	Quick
Carrots, sliced	0–1	Quick
Cauliflower, cut into florets	0–1	Quick
Corn, on the cob	4	Quick
Frozen Cut Vegetables	0–1	Quick
Green Beans	0–1	Quick
Potatoes, cut into 1-inch chunks	4–6	Quick
Spaghetti Squash, halved	7–10	Quick
Spaghetti Squash, whole	15–18	10 minutes
Sweet Potatoes, whole	20–30	Quick
Zucchini	0	Quick

Acknowledgments

I am so grateful for all of the talented and caring individuals who helped make this book possible.

To my editor, Julie Bennett, and my agent, Steve Troha, thank you both for working with me again to bring my third book into the Ten Speed family. I feel lucky to work with such a dream team, and appreciate the support of the entire crew at the Crown Publishing Group and Penguin Random House. Thanks to Emma Campion for your skilled art direction, to Lisa Schneller Bieser for designing such a beautiful book layout, and to Dan Myers for nailing the production. Thank you also to copy editor Amanda Dix, proofreader Ellen Cavalli, and production editor Lisa Regul for your attention to detail when reviewing and perfecting my manuscript.

To the team at Instant Pot, thank you for giving this book your stamp of approval and for your support throughout this entire process.

To my readers and Detoxinista community, this book wouldn't be possible without your daily visits, comments, and emails. You all keep me motivated and inspired, and I am forever grateful for your support and encouragement!

To my volunteer recipe testers, thank you for bravely trying my Instant Pot experiments, both good and bad, and for providing such honest and detailed feedback. These recipes are better because of you.

I couldn't have done it without the help of Karen and Kevin McNellis; Mike McNellis; Sue von Geyso; Courtney and Tucker Gilmore; Sara, Tom, Audrey, and Ian Maples; Kristina and Alex Henton; Laura Sloofman; Zoe Bellinghausen; Wendy Burns; Beth Jelks; Lily Patino; Jennifer Haer; Pam DuBois; Cindy O'Brien-Hallberg; Nicole Cochrane; Melissa Poirier Schnase; Talitha Ellsworth; Joani Rengering Means; Chelsea Rose; Allie Duquette-Fuller; and Kendra Bauman. And a special thanks to my youngest taste testers, Charlotte, Finn, Beckett, and Penny.

To my mom and dad, thank you for your constant love and support. Dad was right when he said he married Mary Poppins! Mom, I couldn't have done this without you, and my kids are so lucky to have you in their lives. (And I'm lucky to have you, too!) You went above and beyond your grandparental duties during this busy time in my life, and I appreciate it more than I can say. I love you both!

To my mother-in-law, Sue, thank you for all of your help, from taste-testing to trying to keep up with my messy kitchen, and, most important, for being "Grand" to my kids. I really appreciate all the extra time you put in to help keep us afloat!

To Marie Radke, thank you for being such an excellent multitasker. I appreciate you taking the time to help me each week, and especially for being my hand model throughout this book.

To my son and daughter, I feel like the luckiest person alive to have you both in my life, and I cherish each moment that we get to spend together. You bring so much laughter and joy into our home! It is because of you that I wanted to create the recipes in this book, so that I could minimize my time in the kitchen and spend more of it with you.

Finally, to Austin, thank you for putting up with our chaotic kitchen, taste-testing my recipe successes and failures, taking care of our son's middle-of-the-night wake-up sessions, and for being the best husband, and father to our children, that I could possibly imagine. You are the most caring, creative, and fun person I know, and I am so lucky that I get to be married to you.

About the Author

MEGAN GILMORE is the creator and recipe developer behind Detoxinista.com, a website that makes healthy living easier and more accessible, and the author of *Everyday Detox* and *No Excuses Detox*. A certified health coach and certified nutritionist consultant, she trained at the Institute for Integrative Nutrition and NHI College. Megan lives with her husband and two children near Kansas City, Kansas.

Index

The information contained in this book is based on the experience and research of the author. It is not intended as a substitute for consulting with your physician or other health-care provider. Any attempt to diagnose and treat an illness should be done under the direction of a health-care professional. The publisher and author are not responsible for any adverse effects or consequences resulting from the use of any of the suggestions, preparations, or procedures discussed in this book.

Library of Congress Cataloging-in-Publication Data
    Names: Gilmore, Megan, 1983- author.
    Title: The fresh & healthy instant pot cookbook: 75 easy recipes for light meals
    to make in your electric pressure cooker / Megan Gilmore.
    Other titles: The fresh and healthy instant pot cookbook
    Description: California: Ten Speed Press, [2018] | Includes index.
    Identifiers: LCCN 2018022147
    Subjects: LCSH: Quick and easy cooking. | Pressure cooking. | Electric cooking,
    Slow. | LCGFT: Cookbooks.
    Classification: LCC TX833.5 .G5364 2018 | DDC 641.5/87—dc23
    LC record available at https://lccn.loc.gov/2018022147

Hardcover ISBN: 978-0-399-58261-5
eBook ISBN: 978-0-399-58262-2

Printed in the United States of America

Design by Lisa Schneller Bieser
Food and prop styling by Megan Gilmore

10 9 8 7 6 5 4 3

First Edition